SECOND EDITION

INVESTING
SHOULD BE EASY

Why Investing Works:
A Practical Guide for the Everyday Consumer

ALEX RICHWAGEN

DEDICATION

To my Dad, who laid the foundation for all my
investment knowledge. He gave me the ability to
communicate that wisdom onto others.
In other words, this is the book he never wrote...
This one is for you Dad,

PREFACE

*T*hink of a revolutionary product. One of my first experiences was with the iPod. I remember early on when the iPod just came out. I had an Intel (INTC) MP3 player at the time and a friend of mine had just bought the iPod. I observed the simplicity of the iPod and compared it to my Intel MP3 player. It was a much better product. Within the next 3-6 months, I slowly saw all of my friends had iPods and it wasn't long until I had one too. At the time, Apple's stock was trading around $10 per share. At that very moment, I should have recognized that Apple was onto something, a massive disruption to the industry. This meant the iPod was exploding onto the scene, and it was ultimately the end of the Walkman and portable CD player. We as consumers knew it was a beautiful game changing product when it arrived. The same thing happened years later with the iPhone. The iPhone would go on as one of the greatest technology enhancements in history. Those are the moments to look out for when it comes to products in life and capitalize on the potential as it relates to the common marketplace. Take that knowledge and understand how to make a smart investment.

Table of Contents

WHAT'S IN THE NEW VERSION?

The markets, economy, and political landscape have changed drastically since the first installment of this book and I felt I had to adjust (plus some feedback from readers helped a lot - thanks!). My overall strategy hasn't changed, but the approach and execution has changed since the first version. This will continue to evolve to adjust with the world. Some pieces of the book flat out just became dated. For example, the brokerage community completely changed with zero trading fees. Other areas of the book just changed so much because of the global economy. We've had days/weeks where the stock market moved more than 10%.

Other examples include the longest bull market ever with 10 consecutive years of growth (albeit some brief dips along the way only to see the market within a period rebound), and the federal bank (the fed) cut the interest rate to almost zero in late 2019. To top it off, a celebrity businessman (Trump) took the White House that almost every political pundit got wrong (Trump beating Hillary in 2016) by every measure, statistic, or political guess. Traditionally, a President, working with both the Senate and the House of Congress, doesn't impact the global economy. This couldn't be further from the truth than what happened from 2016-2020. Among some of the key events of impact are:

- Trade war / Tariff war with China
- Interest rate trending down to 0%
- Stronger pro-business policy (financials were allowed to start increasing dividends)
- New President, new world with 24/7 news cycle – The current President tweets consistently
- Global Trade had a tremendous impact on the global economy, the future and impacting policy. The results were positive for United States, and changed investment into USA companies

- Near zero interest rate environment – making it difficult to achieve any rate of return (bonds) without more money flowing into stocks, driving up stock prices
- More financial firms going into zero based commissions and trading fees.

With all of these changes, I decided version two was a necessity to arm today's investor. So, what really changed in the second version? Well, I'm glad you asked! Lots of improvements, such as:

- A more direct, here's what to do approach
- An update on how the mock portfolios did 5 years later if invested (click here for a sneak peak)
- New mock portfolios with new ideas
- Update on how brokerage accounts modified their policy which altered my recommendations
- Cut out some material that didn't add as much value
- Added strategy for what to do when the markets fluctuate wildly
- Added new strategy on how to find investment ideas
- Put my book on audio book for those that like to listen to books

- AND…A really important piece, I decided to start a weekly investment podcast titled <u>Investing Should Be Easy</u>, with a mailbox for questions – <u>alex.richwagen@gmail.com</u> to subscribe and keep up with all the latest trends, changes in the market, and how to react

All of these areas are littered throughout the book to reflect the positive changes in the investment strategy to make a smarter investor. Any major changes are marked by *HEADS UP BOOK CHANGES AHEAD*, to call attention a significant change to the strategy. So, while reading, if seeing a passage that says *"HEADS UP BOOK CHANGES AHEAD"*, it will signal there is a significant change to the book and investment strategy. I purposefully did this to alert previous readers who own the first version and ease of navigation – hope you like it! Without further ado, let's get back into it. Please remember to send me any questions and subscribe to the <u>podcast, Investing Should Be Easy</u>.

Chapter One

My Personal Story

Regardless of version, I'll always continue to starting off this book off by explaining that at one point in my life, I felt just like you. I didn't understand how investing worked. I think this is best explained with a personal example. Remember back in middle school or high school when the teacher played a trick by asking the class how much money they needed to make it rich? Everyone's thoughts were focused on how rich they were going to become because of how smart they were (and we all believed that smarts were enough to make it rich without all the tools and work, right?). How many people in the class immediately said, "$1 Million Dollars"? Well, count me in as one of the kids that answered it that way. Shortly after, the teacher told us the chances were that only one of the students in the entire class would become rich. Everyone thought deep down that it would be them. So did I.

I want to emphasize one thing before going further. Investing should be viewed as a long-term strategy that will not get people rich quick. It is something that can be learned (as I intend to help lead the way), like how the stock market works in today's economic environment. I know some may be nervous because of the stock market tech bubble in 2000 , the housing market downturn in 2007, and most recent, the Coronavirus COVID-19 in 2020, and I have two words: <u>Don't Worry</u>. My portfolio lived through all of these markets and it is still afloat and doing quite well. The mock portfolios I provided in the first edition 5 years ago returned 86%, 102%, and 107% that depended on which portfolio chosen. There's a reason many folks lost money. They got greedy and didn't stick to a long-term strategy. Regardless of those short term fluctuations, the stock market has returned 11% on average, SINCE 1910!!! We will discuss this further, along with compound interest and how money has the opportunity to double every 7 years. There's an easy way to figure this out that I'll explain later.

This same exact idea of aiming to be a millionaire continued into my college years. After transferring to UCF from Florida State, I eventually found myself in the business side of academics. In my first Intro to Finance class, the first thing the professor asked the entire class of 250 students was, "How many people in this class are already investing?" I nervously put my hand up and quickly realized I was 1 out of 3 students. 3 students out of 250 (>1%). She then proceeded to tell us, "Look around at those individuals with their hands up. They will be the ones wealthy later on in life." I felt so embarrassed on the outside, but strangely confident on the inside about what had just happened. How did she know the three of us would be wealthy later on, and why didn't so many other students raise their hands or know the basics of investing? I want people to feel the same confidence that I did that day and will explain exactly how to do it.

Fast-forward to the present with some ideas or learned some things about saving for the future. Earlier, we talked about those wonderful hopes and dreams that had filled everyone when they were younger. These priorities have probably changed completely with shifts in goals, lifestyle, and income. The new priorities include saving for a new house, starting a family, or putting away money for retirement. After getting past the early 20s, people generally become more focused on goals, responsibility, and planning for the future (if it hasn't happened, don't worry, it will happen). Regardless of the goal, keep the pain in mind (i.e. saving for retirement) with the reward associated with it (i.e. personal satisfaction by removing the fear of either never reaching retirement or even worse, running out of money at some point).

What about the knowledge already stored away? Trust me, I bet it's a lot. Let me give an example. From ages 8-18, my father started teaching me simple concepts far earlier than I cared to know at the time. Even though I tried to drown him out, he was quite persistent. He would cut out newspaper clippings that told stories of two people, where one began investing early and one later. The concepts were easy to understand. The earlier investor always won the race (if viewing retirement as a race). In some magical way, money seemed to grow and double every now and then. I understood those stories, but didn't really understand why it happened.

To put his plan into action, my father suggested that we play a game. He would put $100 into my savings account and $100 into a stock on my behalf, but the only catch was I wasn't allowed to touch either one for an entire year. I thought I was so much smarter, saying the savings account was the obviously better idea because it was very safe. As part of the rules, if I wanted to keep the money, I had to tell him every four months how much each was worth. This was easy enough so I decided to play the game. Here were the results –

- Month 4 – Savings = $100, Stock = $96 (My guess was winning!)
- Month 6 – Savings = $100.25, Stock = $102 (I was slightly losing now)
- Month 9 – Savings = $100.25, Stock = $104.50 (I was losing, but my not much)
- Month 12 – Savings = $100.50, Stock = $113.50 (I definitely lost my guess)

I lost the game, but at least Dad let me keep the money (so I guess he lost). I told him, "Big deal! You only won by $13.00." He laughed at me and said, "It's more important to know the percentage by which you lost vs. the actual amount. Divide the profit from each by 100 to get the answer which is the rate of return." Back then I wasn't concentrating on the rate of return, but more focused on the actual result. This meant far less when dealing with lower sums of money. After realizing that my choice yielded 0.5% and the stock returned 13.5%, the percentages really began to tell a story. This was something I never understood before this exercise. The rate of return isn't something naturally thought about as a kid. It wasn't really until having a 401K plan that a rate of return is even something that I generally hear people talk about in day to day conversations.

Chapter Two

WHAT DO YOU
ALREADY KNOW?

I mentioned before that everyone's knowledge level varies in how much information is understood about investing and finance. The truth is that most people know more than originally thought, as it is just buried within other concepts that drive the foundation of investing. Keep that in mind as we move forward into the next section.

The fact that you were curious enough to pick up this book or even another investment book is a great thing. Congratulations! So many folks in the world today are too intimidated by the idea of stock market investing that they would rather not bother trying. Investing is similar to most topics. By that, I mean how much you need/want to know depends entirely on interest level. The subject of investing goes hand in hand with personal savings with the biggest difference is where the excess money goes towards. Most folks may not even realize how much investment knowledge they currently have. Let's go over a simple examples that's easy to understand. How many out there have ever tried gardening or know anything about it?

INVESTING IS SIMILAR TO GARDENING

How is this possible? Like most things in life, everything starts off with a base level of knowledge, and then expands from there. How much do you know about gardening? I'd assume at least the following basics:

- Seeds are needed to make sprouts and continue to grow to become plants
- Plants must be planted either in the earth or a pot
- Plants can bloom with fruits and flowers, and grow larger
- Most plants need water and sunshine to survive
- Some require lots of attention and some require none at all

Now, that is pretty basic for gardening, so would you consider yourself completely oblivious to gardening or perhaps more of a beginner? I'm assuming everyone would raise their hand as being closer to the beginner's category and admit to at least knowing some of the above information. Think about it; some of this stuff is right there. It just takes a bit of observation and curiosity to recognize it. Let's stick with the gardening example. Becoming more knowledgeable and be on the way to becoming an expert, it's easy to find subjects like:

- Types of plants (orange trees, flowers, shrubs)
- Plant needs (amount of water, how much sunlight, food requirements)
- Plant food (specialty food, fertilizer, organic vs. non-organic)
- Seasonality (which months? Summer vs. winter better to plant?)
- Potting preferences (garden vs. pot, pot type – big or small?)
- Combining all the knowledge into growing crops in certain seasons

These are good examples of understanding with learning concepts. They require research on whether to plant a vegetable garden, grow a specific pepper that needs 3 hours of sunlight, or simply plant a variety of flowers. Getting to the second stage of gardening is exactly where I want everyone to be once finishing this book in terms of investing, right around the intermediate level with enough knowledge to feel comfortable making decisions. There are sections of this book that will give a high level of information and other parts that will break it down step-by-step to hit multiple audiences' interest levels (specifically beginner to intermediate).

Let's go back to the beginner gardener example and bring out the beginner investor by identifying the information already known. Most already have specific tools that to get started on to becoming a more knowledgeable investor. Below we will discuss the following terms – Budgeting, Discretionary Income, Spending Plan, Vacation Planning (Really?), 401K Matching Contribution, Social Security, and Inflation. I'll bet that most have heard of at least a few of those terms that makes this entire process a little less intimidating. Everyone should at least know about Vacation Planning!

BUDGETING

What is a budget? I don't mean the federal one, but a monthly budget to balance expenses vs. income (how much money you make and get to keep). Regardless of whether it's written down, on an excel spreadsheet, checkbook, or just simply not spending more than you make, everyone has a budget of some variation. Very simply put, a budget can be something as easy as balancing expenses against how much money made. An example of John the consumer would be:

- John earns $2,000 per month or $500 per week
- John now have $2,000 to allocate for expenses or saving (taxes are omitted for the example to keep it easier)
- John's main bills (rent, car payment, car insurance, and utilities) are $1,200 per month
- $2,000 - $1,200 = $800 left
- John has $800 in leftover income to pay for things like gas, clothes, food, and saving

DISCRETIONARY INCOME & SPENDING PLAN

The $800 left afterward is what you would call the **discretionary spending**. Let's get more detailed on that. What does that money go towards? Do you have some form of a **spending plan** or is it just spent on whatever? Is there an idea of where the money goes? What about each month; does it fluctuate from month to month? Let me ask some more drilled-down questions with John.

- Did John go out to lunch every day or just once a week?

- Did John go out to dinner? How often?

- When John goes out to dinner, what about drinking alcohol?

- Does John smoke cigarettes?

- Does he go shopping? How often?

- Does he treat himself to a haircut every two weeks? If not, then what about once every four to eight weeks? Manicures or pedicures?

- Does John have a credit card? Is it paid off every month or the minimum payment? This one in specific we will tackle even more later on.

- What does John pay himself?

After all this, is there anything left over? What if John planned for something to be leftover and left it for just him, but in a different account? Looking back over all those questions, here's an idea of the types of extra savings which could quickly begin to add up. Keep in mind, that I'll make assumptions, so these could fluctuate according to personal habits.

- Go out to lunch every day or just once a week? 3 times, extra $20 weekly

- Go out to dinner? How often? 3 times, extra $50 weekly

- When at dinner, is there any alcoholic drinks? 2 drinks x 3 times = $30 weekly

- Smoke cigarettes? 1 pack per week = $8.50 weekly

- Shop for new clothes? How often? = $300 monthly

- Get a new haircut every two weeks? If not, then what about once every four to eight weeks? Manicures or pedicures? $50 month

- Have a credit card? Is it paid off every month or just the minimum payment? Interest at least $50 per month

These are just assumptions, but maybe some of them hit the monthly budget. Add up all the monthly extra cash, and it equals $842.50 per month and $10,110 annually. If any of the above is anything near in all the little extras currently spent, does it equal one big WOW? It's $42.50 over the monthly leftover budget and more (we didn't talk about gas money). The monthly budget just went out the window. Think about the potential savings that are left on the table, add in a very modest 5%, and it's a return of $505.50 annually ($10,110 x .05 = $505.50).

Now I know that's everything inclusive above, but see how quickly it could add up to make small dents in the spending budget and start to pay yourself a little bit each month? Do any of the above situations look like your personal monthly budget or at least one piece that could be potentially relatable? After thinking about some of those answers, start to formulate an idea of a spending plan to go alongside the budget to balance it.

VACATION PLANNING

All of this could be a start to creating or improving the budget. Ever planned a really fun vacation? I can feel you nodding. Think about that type of planning and sacrifice that went into planning the ideal vacation within budget. That's the same type of discipline needed to have in to do what everyone eventually wants to do… EXACTLY WHAT YOU WANT TO DO!

That means retirement and having a plan to get there without working until 76 years old. More importantly, this means enjoying parts of life that's meant for whatever people want to do and not leaving the best years (or all of them) behind. Nowadays, companies set up lots of services such as free investment consultations to help because they realize they can't have the same staff working forever. The point is to make retirement planning to be as serious as vacation planning.

The statement earlier about "what if there is leftover cash" shows that not much is required to get started. This could include some simple re-training of monthly habits, to thinking differently about paying yourself through a spending plan. Stop right there. Re-train? Think about it this way, every time something new comes up in life (join a new class, join a gym, change eating habits, get a pet), the need to re-train planning differently is required.

If it's a new gym membership the plan is to, in some way, account for $40 less per month. Does that mean one less night at the movies or one less night out with the guys/girls for poker? Maybe it does. It's not that hard; it just takes time, discipline, and focus to incorporate changes into the monthly plan. Monthly planning is much easier than long term planning because of situations that occur in life unexpectedly, and that it's short term. Monthly planning is short term planning, and short term is much easier to keep in perspective. Once in the habit of successful budgeting, weeks quickly turn into months of executing the new plan. Soon enough, you'll have 4-6 months booked of successful planning. From there, it will become a routine exercise and won't seem so difficult at all.

Now, how much money do you pay yourself? WHAT?!? "Pay yourself" What exactly do I mean by that? I mean every month you pay bills that goes somewhere else, right? Well, with the leftover cash, do you ever think to pay yourself? Does the extra money stay in the checking or savings account earning .025% interest? That's fine, but think about it in a different way. If you made a $50 payment to yourself in another account, it doesn't sound that crazy, right? That extra account could be a brokerage account. Maybe the idea will take some time to get comfortable…but, at least we are at a starting point. Remember earlier when I talked about the game my Dad played regarding putting money in a savings account vs. investing into a stock. That's the game.

Getting back to vacation. The last vacation you went, how did that budget come to be? Save a little here and there (think back to the spending plan questions). Were you able to accomplish it and go on that vacation (other than credit card debt) by saving in chunks at a time? Can you afford to pay yourself as little as $50 per month? If not, then what about $50 every other month? Every three months? Even at four months it will be $12.50. I'd assume that by some increment along the way you could make a commitment to yourself, set aside the extra money, and do it.

Remember the gardening example? Let's recap just in case you didn't know much about investing and even beginner's knowledge. So far, we covered a budget (expenses vs. income), a spending plan (weekly & monthly spending allowance), and discretionary income (think vacation money). That's a pretty good start to understand how-to start thinking about investing and some foundation to the concept. Let me introduce three more aspects to add to the foundation. These concepts are a 401K matching contribution, social security, and inflation. Do these sound familiar?

401K MATCHING CONTRIBUTION

A **401K matching contribution** is a company match from an employer. It's basically free money all employees are entitled to receive as long as they comply with the necessary requirements (specific percentage contributed is most common). Many companies began adopting 401k plans with matching contributions as an alternative solution to employee retirement savings, as opposed to more expensive pension plans. Remember all the stories years ago of Ford almost going bankrupt? They were 100% true. A very big reason is because of all the guaranteed pension plans to retired workers the company promised (paying someone $80 an hour until they pass away or a big lump sum). The key takeaway is that companies had to adjust and identify another way to contribute to employee retirement savings.

People should expect 401K plans to stick around for the long term. It's a pre-tax investment when contributing until the investor decides to draw from the investments much later in life. What does that mean? It means that the money will grow tax free for a number of years. Once someone begins to draw money from the 401k plan, it does get taxed within the normal tax bracket. The amount of taxes is dependent with each individual on how much is withdrawn and other factors.

Most retirement plans are already setup by the employer. These are some underlying questions to know. Don't know the answers? Then please do the due diligence and go investigate.

- How does the company's 401k plan work?
- How about the 401K matching percentage? This is the amount the company will guarantee to contribute to the 401K retirement plan as long as the employee contribute a specific amount.
- What about the company match in the 401k plan? Odds are that it's somewhere between 3-6% depending on several factors. Find out this percentage given to employees as this is FREE money that could potentially be left on the table.

Please take advantage of this option because if not, it's essentially allowing them to pay less. Think about it. Imagine if every dollar with the matching program invested went down to zero. The company is guaranteed to match the investment up to a specific percentage, meaning no risk. Directly under the same premise of a 401K matching contribution is the employee stock purchase plan.

How can my job help me with my investments or investment strategy? If you didn't go to business school or take any business classes, the following passage may surprise you. Most companies rely heavily on compensating their executives with stock options with the actual salary. A company's top employee's salary is directly tied to the performance of the company, which encourages better results. Now, here's the secret, most employees at publicly traded companies get the same perk. Purchasing company stock at a discount.

EMPLOYEE STOCK PURCHASE PLANS (ESPP)

Most publicly traded companies offer **employee stock purchase plans** that are advertised with a significant discount from the current market price (generally 5-20% discount). If working for a solid publicly traded company with successful products or services, it could become a very successful portion of the investment strategy.

Add into that if the company pays a dividend in the 2-4% range, and the investment could yield a nearly guaranteed 9%-24% annual return. This means if a company pays out a 4% dividend and offers a 5% discount, that's a nearly guaranteed 9% return.

It's not very common to find investments that can nearly guarantee that type of return (since there is no guarantee in any investment). The secret part is that most employees fail to take advantage of this great company benefit and put money away for their own advantage because of the process it takes to do it. The process generally involves multiple steps and is a pain to sign-up. Companies offer this benefit to retain their top talent from going elsewhere. Take the extra 30-60 minutes to research and find out about it or even ask the Human Resources Department how to do it. One last note, don't devote more than 10% of the overall portfolio to one company especially if using this option.

Let me give an example of my story. A former company of mine offered an employee stock purchase plan that gave a 5% discount for purchasing company stock. The company used a transfer agent with 5-6 steps (Computershare) to facilitate the stock transactions. Outsourcing this segment of the business is less expensive than providing the services itself. The plan was open to all employees when I was hired, but the process of setting it up could be really frustrating. Getting started is the trigger (action) that keeps most folks from participating. To register, I had to enroll in the company resource (their online site or external site like Computershare), elect a percentage to be deducted from each paycheck (generally 1-10%), and there may be a few forms to fill out and physically mail in, depending on the transfer agent. The process could take anywhere from 2-4 weeks to setup, which deters people to set it up. I registered in mine from Day One from when I was able to take advantage of the program and utilized that guaranteed return during unstable markets to stabilize my portfolio. After 7 years, the initial $50 per paycheck ballooned to over $20,000 with investment growth.

Let's put this into practice by incorporating a company stock purchase plan into an investment strategy. The next time at work, obtain some helpful information to determine all the questions below. First off, is the company publicly traded? This simply means answering the question, is the company listed on the New York Stock Exchange (NYSE) or NASDAQ.

Unsure? Go to Google.com/finance and lookup the company name. Does the company offer an Employee Stock Purchase Plan (ESPP) or another version? How much of a discount will they provide for investing in their company? Every employee should have a good idea if they work for a company that they would feel comfortable investing in. Start paying attention to those Corporate FYIs, Earnings Release, and general information as they explain exactly how the company is performing.

SOCIAL SECURITY

The next concept of investing knowledge that is already known is **Social Security**. What is Social Security? Social Security is a foundation of economic security for millions of Americans that pay into this as a tax with every paycheck received. It serves to provide monetary assistance to people by using public funds (taxes). The amount each person receives is based on age, income, and Medicare needs. The next paycheck, look at the paycheck details and notice how much money goes to Social Security taxes.

Every single paycheck that's taxed, will have a Social Security Tax (unless making over a certain threshold of earnings). I'm bringing up this concept because it's something already known. Something unknown is by the time retirement arrives, Social Security tax money not be there based on current and historical spending records. Yes, it can and may just go broke within our lifetime. This means planning accordingly is absolutely essential in case that happens.

INFLATION

Inflation is the last item to cover for the knowledge concepts probably already known. To cover the concept of inflation, I want to explain it in a completely different way that will contradict with the government reports. Inflation is basically the rise in prices with a general basket of goods. For example, if the price of milk is $3.25 this year and last year it was $3.00, then the price increased by $0.25. The percentage increase is 8.3%. Inflation isn't really correct in my opinion and let me explain why. The government can interchange out items to make it look more favorable in their own view and public sentiment. Keep that thinking cap on and I'll continue to explain.

As we begin to discuss inflation, investing in general terms, and knowledge points, let's start with the more obvious question, why invest? Well, let me explain why I understood the need to invest. Because leaving money sit in a savings account every year or even those really (ahem) profitable certified deposits (CD's) at a bank doesn't return large returns. Keeping money in a savings account will lose money. Why? Well, the answer is simple. Inflation. It may not feel like truly losing money, but trust me, it's not growing. Think about it logically and think back at least 5-10 years. Are any of the following products listed below more expensive today than 10 years ago?

- Milk
- Eggs
- Bread
- Cereal
- Medicine (any medications?)
- Home prices (mortgage costs)
- Education expenses (College or High School)
- Car prices

Eating at home or at a restaurant has become more expensive since the price of food has slowly risen over the past few decades (as evidence above and the budgeting example). Producing crops is more expensive since fuel and materials are more expensive. Medicine continues to improve the quality of life and is constantly evolving; however, improving the quality of life means people will live longer equating to higher healthcare costs. I remember when I had surgery in 2007 that costs me $100 out of pocket. Today, that same surgery would involve lots of complex billing as hospitals have gotten smarter with breaking each team into sub units meaning they can all individually charge a bill. The old rules that the government will take care of you with social security need to be thrown out. The amount on how much is needed to retire will continue to climb since people will be living longer lives. The need to start embracing the new rules of being self-dependent on self-driven retirement savings is much more important today than ever in history.

One thing people dream about is the reality of owning their own home. This is one of the biggest purchases that many individuals will make by purchasing a house. The prices of houses over the past 20 years have increased without a doubt and so have the requirements set forth by banks to buy a house. Prior to the mortgage crash (and stock market crash) in 2007-08, the rules and restrictions on buying a house were less regulated. Now, because of the crash and the irresponsibility shown by banks, underwriters, and mortgage lenders, there are much higher degrees of scrutiny and costs to buying a house. Just like the hospitals, all the people in the supply chain get paid increasing costs.

One major change in the past 10-15 years is banks requiring much higher down payments, at least 20 percent, to guarantee the loan against PMI (Private Mortgage Insurance). What's 20 percent of a median house, averaging $200,000? $40,000. How many currently have $40,000 lying around or want to borrow the 401K tomorrow? Most folks today probably don't want the 401k hit or have this amount available to contribute to a potential house purchase. As a result, more and more people are waiting longer to buy a house and start a family. Younger generations are putting off starting a family and buying homes triggered by a number of factors.

What about education, do kids (assuming you have them) need a computer or iPad now instead of paper and pencils? What about you? Attending graduate school or finishing a degree? Maybe those basic items are still needed (paper and pencil), but the technology costs for education keep increasing the overall financial impact. Computers, laptops, and tablets are staples when it comes to education nowadays and appear to be in the foreseeable future. College tuition is a whole new ballgame. College tuition has risen over 500% since 1985. Data from the Consumer Price Index (CPI) shows inflation has been quite stable year over year (or so the government basket of goods says so) in the same time period, but college tuition is really soaring out of control. Is there anything else that has dramatically increased this stretch more than tuition? Look at this chart provided by <u>Us News</u> from 2000-2020 (that was even worse 40 years ago in 1980)

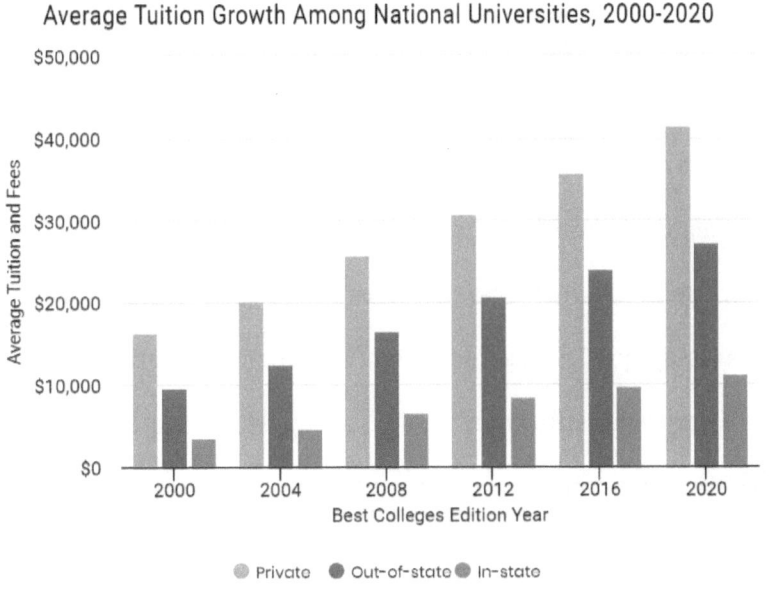

Average Tuition Growth Among National Universities, 2000-2020

Think about the 500% increase in college tuition in context. If tuition was in the CPI, then a $10,000 tuition in 1985 should be around $20,000 today. This is obviously not the case as that same college tuition and education in 1985 is approaching $50,000 today. The main reasons for the increase, cited by schools, is to continually renovate buildings to provide research and computer labs.

The average undergraduate student completes their education with about $20,000 in student debt. The average graduate school is an additional $30,000. Even the $30,000 estimate is increasing year over year. For example, I attended the University of Central Florida, UCF, for my graduate degree from 2010-2012, with a total cost of $33,500 (early acceptance took $1,500 off the initial cost of $35,000). *Check with the registrar to see if this option if attending graduate school to lower expenses.* In 2020, the cost had already risen to $39,000 in a short period of time. More money, more expenses.

The last piece of inflation involves owning a car and car insurance as a rising cost. As a society, the American population is by far and large a car ownership society at all ages past the legal driving age of 16. Many other countries rely on either public transportation (trains, subways, light rail) or other types of transportation like bicycles or mopeds, at a much higher frequency. Car prices seem to be one to hone in on here given gas prices have remained steady with the price of oil crashing. All of these examples of rising costs all lead to the same point.

Basically, I'm trying to point out that inflation comes in many different forms. It simply cannot beat it by leaving money sitting in a savings account.

The main point above that I have illustrated about inflation is it comes in several forms. Let's tackle inflation alone and run it against a current salary. For example, let's use $50,000 as the annual salary. If that money stayed in a checking account and generates .25% with prices that keep rising over time, it will earn less. If that $50,000 annual salary gets a raise of 2%, and inflation is at 4% to be modest, and the bank provides .25% interest rate, it's actually down -1.75% overall. Let's go through an example and pretend there's $10,000 in the bank account. The actual new $52,000 actually is less. Here's how it works:

$50,000

X   .02 (2% raise)

_____

1,000 (raise increase)

  +25 (checking interest with 10k x .25%)

  -2,000 (inflation) (50k x .04)

_____

  -975 total

That's crazy right? The fact we got a raise, earned more money, the raise wasn't even taxed (yet), and the total still results negative for the annual year. How is that possible? Let's revisit the inflation term and describe where it comes from before we move forward. **_Remember, it's not how much you make, but it's how much you get to keep_**.

Inflation is officially is defined by the government and their "magic" formula used is calculated by the Consumer Price Index (CPI), which produces inflation numbers. To understand more information with the calculations , go to www.bls.gov/cpi. My guess is for most people, the explanation is unnecessary, but I wanted to at least provide the resource just in case.

CAN YOU EVEN AFFORD TO INVEST?

Every person must assess their own circumstances to determine whether or not to invest depending on their own situation. The first question to assess is can you actually afford to invest? Start by going through all finances and most importantly, assess any outstanding debt with the interest rate. Those interest rates are really important factors in the ability to invest.

Have debt? If the interest rate is below 6%, that's a green light to signal there's room to invest. If the interest rate is over 6%, it's probably best to pay down the loan first. Why 6%? Most loans have compounding interest, meaning the percentage quoted is often lower than the actual interest rate to be paid. Check any of the loans that are current. Check the fine print. How many of them compound daily, monthly, or quarterly? What about resetting? Loans are a very sophisticated product and it's easy to get caught off guard without going through the fine print. Here's a quick story of why this is important.

A few years back, I purchased a boat and financed the purchase instead of paying all in cash. After several weeks of researching, test driving, and getting loan quotes, I found a 5.3% interest rate through Light Steam. This was a fantastic rate. The rate however on the surface was 5.3%; however, if I kept the loan the entire 4 years, it compounded daily and readjusted quarterly (very slick underwriting). *The interest rate ended up being 11.8% after all the creative math*!!!! As a result, I went ahead and paid off the loan because it's easier to beat the market at 5.3%, not over 11.8%.

All this said, if now is not the right time to make investment decisions because of debt given a loan's interest rate, then perhaps in the next year or two would be more appropriate. Here are a few basic financial questions to see if there are other pressing needs that should be taken care of first:

- Have credit card debt?
- What about student loan debt?
- What about a car payment?

These are the three biggest sources of personal debt (outside of a mortgage) that restrict earnings potential with investments. Always remember, it's not how much you make, but it's how much you get to keep. *You will continue to hear this again to emphasize the point*. If answering yes to any of the questions above, what type of interest rate is it?

- Credit Cards – As of July 2020, the average credit card Annual Percentage Rate (APR) was 19%, according to wallethub.com. This means on average anyone keeping a balance on a credit card will pay more than 19% on the debt (APR is compounded monthly = higher rate).

- Student Debt – As of July 2020, the average student loan rate is 5.8%. This can fluctuate according to different terms and conditions (could start when graduated, or years later, etc.).

- Car Payment – As of July 2020, the average rate is 5.3% dependent on credit and the length of the loan (72, 60, 48, 36 month car loan).

Is the interest rate anywhere close to these statistics? Take a look at the contract to find out the interest rate owed. Remember the stat given earlier about the stock market returning an average of 11% per year since 1910? Depending on the rate, it may be smarter to pay down debt first before embarking on the investment adventure. It doesn't make much sense to try and earn 11% return with risk, if there's a debt obligation ranging close to 15%.

For example, let's say I owe $4,000 on 7% annual APR (actual 7.23% because the rate escalates due to monthly compounding), I'd owe $4,289 and the interest keeps running. This is because a portion goes to principal and the rest goes towards interest depending on the contract. If it's possible to pay off the loan of the car at $4,000, it saves the remaining $289 interest owed. This isn't a book on debt management, but I thought the example would help with making decisions. *As a rule of thumb, if outstanding debt owed is at least 6%, pay off the debt first.*

DIFFERENT INVESTMENT OPTIONS

Let's address the a possible question that may be lingering... why invest money in the stock market vs. other options? The answer to the market is to beat inflation often. Here's some alternatives to the market to briefly cover the topic.

- Real Estate
- Private Business (personal, friends, or angel investing)
- Valuable Art & Collectibles (paintings, antiques, old guns, etc.)
- Precious Metals (gold & silver coins, diamonds)

- CD's at a bank

Let's discuss and review these options one at a time –

- Real Estate – Within real estate there are two main strategies, using real estate for income or actually flipping the property to turn a profit. Start-up capital, knowledge, and experience are required if flipping houses. Typically, lots of money is also required for a down payment, repairs, and upgrades to the property. This doesn't even take into account closing costs and a safety net because essentials in houses break (water heater, dryer, roof). Many people have had significant gains in real estate, but as the cover states, this book is about stock market investments. The money invested will be held for long periods of time as well. Generally, a complex understanding of real estate is needed, if not, it could be a costly lesson.

- Private Business – at least once in life, a friend will ask to invest money in their start-up business and become an investor, just be careful. Usually friends and business don't mix because of the emotional attachment to money. In general, it's difficult to get the money back quickly if at all due to contracts. If investing in a private business, this may not be the wrong book.

- Valuable Art & Collectibles – Just like real estate, there's a significant learning curve to get started and put knowledge into action. Without the proper background, this is a dangerous area to invest due to fraud or understanding true value.

- Precious Metals – Same thing as valuable art and collectibles

- Bank CD's – There is less risk in investing in a bank cd than the stock market. Also, there are many potential downsides to this investment vehicle. A bank certified deposit generally carries a small guaranteed return between 0.5 – 3.0% depending on the current market environment and lending rates. The bank will keep the deposited money for at least 12-28 months, which impacts the rate of return. Breaking the contract with the bank can result in penalties with loss of the return promised. Lastly, liquidity in CD's are very limited due to the fact that the money is locked up without many alternatives.

To sum up all of these other investment vehicles, there are high learning curves and lots of experience needed with 3 out of 5 of them. As opposed to stocks, all five alternatives require the investor to keep the money locked up for long periods of time. Investments in the stock market do not have this same constraint whereas the positions can be sold three days after initial purchase. Even precious metals and paintings will take time to locate a seller, create a fair deal, and facilitate the deal. Let's dig deeper into the markets to provide more foundation.

Chapter Three

STOCKS, MUTUAL FUNDS, ETFs, AND RISK

S tocks are classified as equities or publicly traded companies (I will use these interchangeably) that can be purchased and sold in an open market format. To purchase or sell them, <u>a brokerage account is required</u> for individuals to process the transactions. I mentioned above about the liquidity of stocks, here's how liquid I meant. After a purchase or sale, stocks settle (are available in cash) two days after the initial buy or sale (T+2). T+2 means the stock was bought on T (Trade Date) and settles in two days (+2). Stocks do not have restrictions on the sale at any time after the two business days have passed. If the owner (person who purchased the stock) needs the money, it's available within two business days.

When selling a stock, there are tax consequences. Simply put, if it was owned less than a calendar year and a profit is made, there are higher reportable (to the IRS) tax consequences for that sale. If more than a year, there are lower consequences. These tax consequences are known as capital gains (if a profit) and capital losses (if a loss). I will be addressing more about investing tax strategies later in the book in more detail. Once an individual decides to purchase a specific stock, they effectively become an owner of that company with specific rights:

- Limited Liability – As an owner, there's limited liability in the event something negatively happens to the company
- Evidence of Ownership – Each stock holder is an owner in the company
- Transferability – The shares owned can be gifted to another person or entity
- Inspection – Ability to review books and records (reports are generated and sent to shareholders when the fiscal year is completed)

DIVIDENDS AND FOREIGN NON-DOMESTIC STOCK (ADR'S)

Companies that are more mature (generally at least 5-10 years old) tend to issue dividends. Dividends are payments or shares distributed to shareholders to distribute excess net profit. The money can either be paid out in cash or reinvested back into stock. Dividends are paid and determined by the Board of Directors and are not guaranteed. I'll expand into dividends further in Chapter 5 by going into more detail about them and their tax consequences. Dividends can be issued both domestically and internationally regardless of the location of the company. One thing to note, most of the topics within this book will concentrate on domestic stock ownership concentrated in the US.

Foreign stocks are not much different as far as the actual trade to the end investor. Foreign stocks are traded as American Depository Receipts or ADRs for short. Basically, these are setup for investors to easily trade foreign stocks on US Stock Exchanges. The ADR is priced in U.S. dollars, pays dividends in U.S. dollars, and trades on the major exchanges just like domestic stocks in the United States. One note, is these is a bit of currency risk (currency fluctuations) since the ADR does symbolize indirect ownership of a foreign security.

Additional note – Owning foreign securities can be a great strategy at times. During 2000-2010, the U.S. dollar was annually devalued several times versus other foreign currencies. This means exchanging U.S. dollars for most currencies would receive less money during the exchange. Also, if a foreign stock issued a dividend (Royal Dutch, RDSA, for example), it would pay higher in the USA if the issuing company's currency value was higher. Similarly, if selling a foreign security, ADR, the proceeds would be slightly higher if the exchange rate held firm as it would be paid in U.S. dollars.

WHY DO COMPANIES ISSUE STOCK?

To raise money, a corporation can either finance debt or use equity financing. Equity financing is raising money by issuing stock to shareholders that they in return become owners of the company. Companies issue stock to construct new buildings, expand operations, buy equipment, or just simply scale the business beyond its current production. If the company excel, then the shareholders enjoy in the success of profits with dividends and share value increase. This is how stock ownership works.

Let me provide an example of why companies issue stock in easier context. Let's say Joe the Farmer generally sells on a weekly basis 50 pounds of corn, 50 pounds of wheat, and 50 gallons of milk from his farm. This has been consistent for about three years since Joe started to sell products directly from his farm. Well, for the past three years, all of his supply would generally run out by Saturday afternoon. Over the past two months, Joe's business has picked up through word of mouth, and his supply is gone by Thursday sometimes even Wednesday.

To keep up with customer demand, Joe needs more farmland and a bigger barn to house more animals. Joe has a great track record of paying all his bills on time, but really needs one of the neighboring lands to expand his business. Joe barters a deal with his neighbors Fred, Mike, and George. The deal is that Joe will buy some of the excess land over time, but must give the neighbor a portion of the profits (like a dividend with a stock) going forward in exchange for use and eventual purchase of the land. As the business grows and Joe becomes more profitable, so do his neighbors as they enjoy in the profits at same time. Joe's situation is the same type of scenario to how corporations expand.

MUTUAL FUNDS

Mutual Funds are another investment most should be familiar with as 401K plans are fairly common. Most 401K plans are built with a collection of mutual funds that the company has selected through a provider. Mutual funds are a basket of stocks (100s to 1000s) that a fund manager has strategically selected to diversify risks. This is done to provide individuals a balanced portfolio to reduce potential risk by having stocks from different asset classes and sectors. In general rule, I stay away from Mutual Funds because ETFs (Exchange Traded Funds) are a better alternative. Let's discuss risk.

One common measure of risk that many analysts use is called **beta**. It's one of several measures of risk and provides a high level good start to understanding the company risk vs. the market. It can easily be found by looking at the summary or statistical data on financial sites Finance.Google.com, Finance.Yahoo.com, Finviz. com. Here's how it works. The mid-point or the average for most stocks is 1.0 and it ranging from .5 and over 2.0. As a point of reference, if the beta of the security is greater than 1.0, there is a higher risk than the average stock. Similarly, if the beta for a stock is below 1.0, there is inherent lower risk.

For example, American Express (AXP) common stock has a beta above 1.0 (1.1 as of April 2020) for its average risk because of all their specific company factors taken into consideration (see screenshot below from Finviz.com – my favorite FREE site for several fundamental ratios). That means, AXP is deemed a slightly higher risk than the average investment. Again, if the beta of the security is less than 1.0, there is a lower estimated risk in the security. Risk naturally translates into a measure of reward and how much risk as the investor, you are willing to tolerate. If risk adverse (like most people), then I'd advise selecting securities around 1.0 or less than 1.0. It's that simple, so don't let it be confusing. Unfortunately, most investors want the greatest return with the lowest risk creating an interesting internal dilemma. **Beta = Measure of Risk**. Now that we have a better understanding of risk, let's resume the discussion regarding ETFs.

EXCHANGE TRADED FUNDS (ETFS)

Exchange Traded Funds (ETFs) are the better looking cousin to mutual funds and act in the same manner as a mutual fund as it pertains to a basket of stocks. Why is that, do you ask? Well, ETFs are very similar to mutual funds with comparable compositions. They are constructed to spread out risks by offering a basket of stocks that is selected by a fund manager. The basket of stocks can at times mirror major indexes like the S&P or Dow Jones Industrial Average or selected industries. But still, why are they the better looking cousin?

The hidden secret on mutual funds is the amount in fees that are charged. You may tell yourself that 1.0-3.0% or less isn't much for a mutual fund to charge, but what if I said the average person investing in mutual funds can spend over $150,000 through their life in mutual funds fees. WOW! This number is factored with compound interest over time and what could have been earned instead of given away. Now that I gave a much bigger number to work with, it may be wise to reconsider giving away that 1-3% to a mutual fund. ETFs charge a fraction of that to provide customers with a similar balance of risk in the neighborhood of .25% and offer the same type of returns. Keep this product in mind for later when we get into building a mock portfolio.

INVERSE ETFS

There is another security type under the ETFs category called Reverse ETFs. In 2020, these products became very important as the market tanked due to the Coronavirus COVID-19. Instead of watching the portfolio tank, this is key resource to changing the strategy and protect the portfolio. They are exactly what they sound like, a bet against the index or sector they represent and market going up as a whole. Similar to shorting a stock (predicting that a stock will go down), the same can be done today with an ETF that can serve as a hedge if the market suddenly turns upside down. This can be a great strategy instead of selling off many positions vs. keeping them due to tax implications. I provide some of these examples (For example, DOG & PSQ) in the end of the book located in the index just in case the market turns upside down due to a market correction. They can be found just as easy by typing "Reverse ETF" in a Google search. Just understanding the basics of the reverse investment as an option to hedge the portfolio can be a useful possibility. One last note, I ***highly recommend against*** buying Ultra Short ETFs at 2x and 3x because if the market doesn't correct or goes back up, it will multiply quickly.

BONDS

A bond is a loan whereas the investor is the lender and company the borrower. Bonds offer a much clearer indication of the potential return as the details are provided on the issue. The issuer of the bond, which can be a government entity or business, promises to pay the money back when the bond matures and comes due. A typical loan is about 5-10 years for a corporation or government to pay back the loan in full plus interest. The government and companies issue bonds frequently to raise money for building roads, parks, or even construct a new factory. Issuing debt (bonds) is referred to as leverage financing because the issuer is borrowing against its net worth.

When entities issue bonds, individuals just like you and me can loan them money for a specified return on the investment. Bonds can be bought on the open market just like a stock and has a defined rate of return that is clear to the investor. Bonds are rated on safety/risk from a scale from C to AAA, whereas C is the most risky, and AAA is the safest. Municipal bonds have different types of rating, but are similar in nature. The higher risk equals a lower rating similar to higher risk stocks mean a higher potential return. Bonds are generally recommended as a fixed income product when people approach retirement because they cannot afford to risk any loss of principal (principal is the initial investment). I cover bond ratings and types in further detail in the index and tax sections.

OPTIONS

An option is a contract with the right to buy or sell (not obligated) an underlying security on the market with an offsetting party. The contract details the specific strike price (the price to buy the security), how long the contract is good for (the date it expires), and premium (amount) paid to the offsetting party for the right to buy or sell. The ability to buy or sell options requires an options agreement under a brokerage account because additional prerequisites are mandatory. Options are a more sophisticated investment option for advanced investors and will not be recommended at any point in this book. Consider options a stay away from a beginner's or intermediate standpoint since they require much more diligence.

MONEY MARKET FUNDS

This type of investment option is provided in every brokerage account that exists today. Money Market Funds act as a stable investment alternative when money is sitting pending and not invested. Money cannot just be idle in a brokerage account. As a result, money that isn't being used is automatically purchased into the money market fund of choice. This is very similar to the "savings account" of the brokerage account. When originally setting up a personal brokerage account, the company will give a choice for which fund to use, and it can be changed at any time by simply investing in another. Below are some characteristics of these funds -

- Short term debt instruments – Most money market funds have short term (less than 18 months) debt included in them where most of the debt matures in one year or less.

- Safety of principal and liquidity – The funds are highly safe in regards to risk and are also extremely liquid (can be sold or liquidated easily).

- Provide investors with a stable alternative pending an investment decision – again acts like a savings account while money sits idle and is not invested.

- What's in them? –
    o Treasury Bills
    o Banker's Acceptance notes (facilitate foreign trade)
    o Commercial Paper (unsecured corporate debt)
    o Negotiable CDs (unsecured bank debt)

- o Repurchase Agreements (dealer selling securities to another dealer with agreement to repurchase)
- All above items can make up the money market fund

Now that we have a general understanding of other investment options that are available, let's move forward with the discussion. The next section starts to explain how investing can become very effective to help reach financial goals. Common financial goals consist of retirement, buying a house, paying for college, or anything else that requires a large investment of hard earned money.

Chapter Four

Doubling Money in Seven Years & Compound Interest

This chapter details how an initial investment can increase rapidly over time, but <u>only if it's allowed</u> to grow. This is all possible with the magic of compound interest. Most stocks with enough time will see increases in value, which is the primary reason diversification is so important. It really does make the difference on the potential Return on Investment (ROI) between hundreds of thousands of dollars. Yes, that's right, I said hundreds of thousands could be the difference when starting an investment plan early (early to mid-20s for example) versus even a little bit later (30s and 40s).

The difference is time to allow the investments to grow. At an early age, time is heavily on your side for an investment to grow if and only if the investments are left alone. Let's get back to compound interest and how it works and why it's so important. An important point to remember with compound interest is that the interest gained on the principal continues to grow with the original principal investment. As the amount compounds on itself, it will continue to grow for years at an accelerated rate due to the compound interest. Even Albert Einstein said compound interest is the most powerful force in the world, calling it the 8th wonder of the world. For example, if an investment of $100 earns $10 the first year, the next year the amount starts at $110 and keeps growing. Compound interest and the time value of money go hand in hand.

TIME VALUE OF MONEY

Let me further explain and give an example of compound interest and the time value of money. Let's begin by introducing our two friends, Charlie & Larry. Charlie and Larry will be used throughout the rest of the book as our examples upon investing. Charlie is a very attentive student learning about investing, and Larry tends to procrastinate concerning any advice of investing. Charlie went on Amazon.com per his father's advice and purchased a simple how-to book on investing. Charlie quickly began to digest and understand the book because of the simple concepts to investing.

He learned so much that he bought another copy for Larry. Charlie read this book in his 20s, and Larry procrastinated and didn't have any interest in reading it until he was in his 30s. When Charlie was 21, he took $1,000 and per the instructions, he invested into a few Exchange Traded Funds (ETFs) and stayed to the principles learned, having never sold the investment. The stock market averaged the same rate of return that it has since 1910 and grew at 11%.

- After one year, Charlie's investment grew by 11% and beginning in year two he was left with $1,110 (1000 x 1.11).
- After year two, the investment grew again by 11% to $1232.10 (1110 x 1.11)
- Year three it continued the growth giving him $1367.63 (1232.10 x 1.11)
- And year four it was $1518.07 (1367.63 x 1.11).

Wow, after just four years, the total return was $518.07 along with the $1000.00 in principal. In year seven, after the trend kept up, the original $1000.00 was now $2076.16. Charlie found it amazing that the money really did double in seven years. In 20 years, the original investment would eventually be worth $8062.31. In 40 years, it would be worth $65,000.87. Without investing another dollar, Charlie turned $1,000 into $65,000. He started to wonder if he invested more. This is the magic of compound interest on full display. It only worked for Charlie since he didn't ever touch the original money and let it grow. What happened to Larry, though?

Larry eventually began reading the book Charlie bought for him and didn't start investing until he was 31, a good ten years behind Charlie. Larry thought he was always smarter than Charlie. He decided he would double the amount Charlie invested and put in $2,000 to start. Well, Larry had $5,678.84 in ten years from the original investment and thought he was doing great. Since he only had 30 years to let it grow as opposed to Charlie because he started later at age 31, his ending investment at the same age of 61 was $45,784.59.

Larry thought he was much smarter because he put in double the money than Charlie had originally invested. Larry's confusion was that he ended up with less in the end. What happened here? Well, the answer is in the magic of time and compound interest. The extra ten years allowed Charlie's smaller investment to grow at a much faster rate, while Larry kept waiting to get started with his personal investment plan. Years later, Larry went back to the same investment book and tried to find out what happened.

GOLDEN RULE OF 72 — WHAT IT IS AND HOW CAN IT HELP YOU?

There is the investment rule called the Golden Rule of 72 that I want to introduce. It explains how investing money can double in value from the original amount. This rule is directly related to the rate of return the investment yields. In the above example, since we used the standard stock market rate of return of 11%, we take the golden rule of 72 and divide it by 11 and that yields an answer of 6.5455. Basically, this tells us that the original money investment will double every 6.5 years according to the rule.

If the market rate of 11% continues in the future, the original amount of money will quadruple in value after 13 years (6.5 years x 2) to continue on the path. For example, an initial investment of $1,000 would be worth $4,000 in 13 years with a ROI of 11%, similar to the story with Larry and Charlie. This is precisely why it's important to get started earlier with investing to provide as much time as possible for the investment to grow with compound interest.

Since we now know this magical formula and how powerful it is, why aren't more people taking advantage of this knowledge? If everyone knew about this, then why don't more people use this information and invest? The first reason stems from the background and desire to understanding investment strategy. Beyond the traditional answer of not wanting to understand or spend the time, there are other reasons why people aren't realizing a higher ROI in their lives and portfolios.

HEADS UP BOOK CHANGES AHEAD

REASONS PEOPLE AREN'T REALIZING THEIR FULL INVESTMENT POTENTIAL

- There are many fundamental reasons why most people are not earning their full potential. I'd like to review three of the top reasons in further detail. The reason why it's important to review these is to avoid the unnecessary mistakes to help earn full potential. Among the reasons are spending too much (living beyond current means), attempting to time the market, and trading fees. Let's these discuss in specific detail below.

- Reason #1 - More people aren't doing better because the majority of society is much more like Larry. They start saving later and place higher value on spending money today for the immediate gratification of buying what they want (new cars, clothes, phones, etc.). Wants supersede needs. The values of saving or investing for the future just like Larry falls short. Just think about this concept for a minute. How many people within the immediate circle of friends / family are terrible with money? They seem to always be living paycheck to paycheck (having just enough to cover expenses, barely) and seem to struggle with budgeting at any degree. I can name people in my circles that fall into this trap and saw their struggles firsthand. There is also the funny (or not so funny) example of someone in your network that owes money. That same person is out on a Friday night really living it up. A very close friend of mine is a financial genius when it came to companies and other people's money, but didn't have the required discipline to manage their own. I also have some friends that are now on the path to riches, due to the much of the same information provided in this book.

- Reason #2 – People try to time the market too much. This basically means they wait for the best time to buy stocks and the best time to sell them. It is nearly impossible to time the stock market today for the everyday consumers. Most of us all have regular jobs, are far too busy, and are generally too occupied to watch the stock market every day. Even the geniuses on Wall Street or those folks on MSNBC don't perfectly time the market. They are reacting to the news and coming up with news slants to drive attention with ratings. If this is true, then why does the average person that just read some stock books think they can as well? Good question. Send me an email when you have that answer. If the neighbor or cube-mate brags about a hot stock tip, do yourself a favor, and ignore it and run away. A common behavioral tendency that doesn't help with trying to time the market is viewing investments emotionally (just like gambling). On the flip side, when selling for a loss, it becomes emotionally difficult to rid of the stock because the natural intuition says to wait until it goes back up and to even buy more (doubling down). Unfortunately, in both examples we are acting on emotion and intuition. To really understand why emotions shouldn't run the portfolio, let me provide a brief example of why it shows how difficult it is to recoup the initial investment of a large loss.

o   Stock A – Bought at $20, goes up to $30 - $10 per share gain (50% gain)

o   Stock B – Bought at $20, goes down to $10, losing half of the investment (50% loss)

How much does Stock B have to go back up to recoup the original investment? For those of who said $10, that's correct. Now, more importantly what percentage is that? $10/$10 = 100%! Wow, that's a lot. How many stocks go up 100% very quickly? Very few investments that I can name off the top of my head qualify. Is it more clear why doubling down on a stock can be a bad idea? Remember, there's always a strategy to investing regardless of the ups or downs of the market (reduction of taxes for example).

- Reason #3 – Fees, fees, and more fees. This is a major component in reducing the potential annual return on investment (ROI). Remember the statistic given earlier about mutual funds taking over $150,000 from the average investor over their lifetime (I wasn't kidding). It's the primary reason why in my recommendations to utilize ETFs vs. Mutual Funds within the portfolio. The typical ETF fee is .25% vs. the average mutual fee 1.0%. The difference with compound interest and the difference of the .75% equates to lots of lost capital in the long run. I want to emphasize that over the course of a lifetime, this will continue to add up and shrink the potential investment portfolio.

Author's side note – There are several reasons why people decide to write books, blogs, and/or articles. My initial reason for this specific book was the countless times I have met with someone for 1-2 hours to discuss how investing strategy works. The need to make money work for YOU. Pay yourself first. Simple concepts that will help in the long run. As seen on the dedication page in the beginning, it's the book that my Dad never wrote, since he laid my foundation. The next sections will elaborate on the two growth components to fully realize an investment potential. **Capital appreciation** (by not selling) and **dividends** with how to manage them.

CAPITAL APPRECIATION & DIVIDENDS

Capital appreciation is defined as the increase in value of an asset based on the growth in its market price and value. Remember our example last chapter with Charlie? His initial investment of $1,000 grew at 11% and in Year 2, he was then starting at $1,110. That extra $110 is the example of capital appreciation. When the excess growth ($110) comes from base investment ($1,000), it can continue to grow as long as there's no sale. Remember the concept of investments doubling every 7 years with the Golden Rule of 72? To allow this to happen, it's recommended to not sell the investment. A few pages back, we started to introduce our characters, Charlie and Larry, and reasons why the majority of people don't realize their investment potential. It's clear Charlie was more successful with the main reason being time. Time for the investment to grow and not selling the asset. Larry started later and didn't have as much time on his side. Capital appreciation is the first of the major two sources of return on investment sources. The second is major source is dividends.

Rather than just go straight into defining dividends, how about another story to fully appreciate the value of why dividend reinvestment is so important. Ever heard about Warren Buffet? Even at a novice level, most should know that he is one of the most successful investors. Ever heard the story about Warren Buffett and the famous conference with doctors he hosted back in the 1960s? He explained how to identify growth investments and their long term impact by allowing dividends to keep re-investing into more stock vs. taking the cash dividend. Basically, the story goes like this. Warren Buffett held a prestigious conference with a group of doctors promising to teach them about investing and how to rapidly increase their portfolios under his guidance. He described to his audience of doctors by investing in stable growing companies that regularly paid dividends, it speeds up the capital appreciation to much higher levels. The doctors wanted to know how it was possible. He then went on to further explain the magic of compound interest with dividends as a great multiplier in long term growth.

The story continues that a $3,000 investment in 40 years eventually turned into $300 million. No, I'm not kidding, $300 million. The companies included the likes of Coca-Cola, McDonald's, and Proctor and Gamble. Companies that experienced very high sustained growth patterns for long periods of time. They were able to accomplish this as they scaled their operations across the United States and eventually abroad to other countries. When mature companies have started to establish themselves within their marketplace and are growing at a reasonable pace, they naturally develop an excess in cash flows. Depending on where a company is in their life cycle (Introductory, Growth, Maturity, or Decline), the Board of Directors make decisions such as what to do with the excess cash flow. There are a few general options for the use of the excess cash –

- Pay off debt – If the company had issued bonds, they could retire them early or any other outstanding debt used to expand operations. Since debt is generally cheap, most companies choose not to exercise this option.

- Stock buy-back – If the company thinks their prospects of growth can obviously propel past the current stock price (if they feel it's undervalued), the company could choose to buy its own outstanding shares in the marketplace.

- Invest – If the company is still growing at a high pace (at least over 20% annually), they could re-invest the funds back in the business such as: open another location, expand the product or services internationally, or introduce another product.

- Pay Dividend – If companies get to a maturity point, where it feels all three objectives have been met, they could return the money to shareholders in the form of either a cash or stock dividend to both common and preferred stockholders.

Once companies start to regularly pay dividends, they continue for the foreseeable future creating a known cash flow model. In the Product Life Cycle (see below), this occurs most frequent in the maturity or decline stage, providing the investor with stable expectations. Dividends are normally paid quarterly and most companies increase the dividend amount over time. For anyone not familiar with the product life cycle and the various stages, here is a quick chart to help explain the cycles each and every company goes through in the Product Life Cycle.

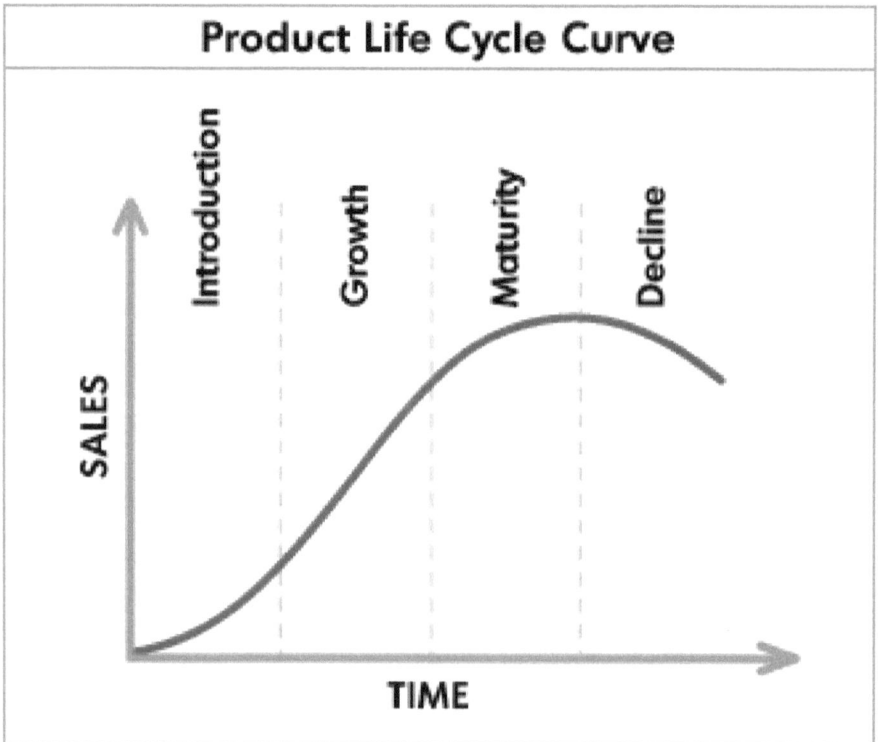

The first two phases are how all companies start off without a specific timeframe on how long they will be in the Introduction or

Growth phase. Can you think of at least a few companies off hand that are in these cycles with high growth into the marketplace? How about Tesla (TSLA) and Netflix (NFLX)? These companies experienced rapid growth in their initial 3-5 years and their stock reflected that growth with high returns to investors. Once companies have a consistent business model and sales cycle, they begin to move into a different phase of the product life cycle. A consistent growth rate could be as common as 10-20%. A few characteristics of this next phase (Maturity) are a fully developed core product and customer base whereas they deliver results routinely. By investing in mature companies, investors know they can count on stable growth, consistent dividend payments, and lower risk in their portfolio. Maintaining a balanced portfolio with dividend paying stocks helps to reduce overall risk.

It's very important to emphasize that in the early investment years (ages 20-40) to always allow stock dividends to re-invest that purchases more stock. Without having any **real prominent need to receive the dividends being issued, allowing the dividends to re-invest is essential to a long term growth**. More stock equals. The dividends will routinely buy more stock and continue to grow into additional capital appreciation. This is an excellent strategy to ultimately help reach financial goals (retirement, buying a house, saving for college) faster because the money has a chance to multiply. This is how capital appreciation works with dividends.

Chapter Five

Practical Guide to Choosing a Brokerage Account

HEADS UP BOOK CHANGES AHEAD

The next section has drastically changed in such a short period of time since the first version of my investment book. I didn't think I'd be writing in 2000, the average price per trade (buy or sell) average $10-$15, trended closer to $7-$10 per trade in 2010, and now two decades later, the average price per trade is down to $0 per trade. Yes, that's correct $0 per trade. Why and what happened? There are several reasons as the financial landscape has changed, existing companies have changed strategies, and new competitors have emerged. The upstart companies that emerged have disrupted the industry by offering low to no cost on trading. The key is the companies had to respond to a growing trend by putting in new cost-effective strategies.

New brands have started to emerge. These brands have something going for them that previous brokerage houses didn't have the luxury to do. They don't have a need to purchase a large building, don't required large volumes of employees, and are strictly digital. Brands like Robinhood, Acorns, or Ally Bank Invest have come into the marketplace with low overhead resulting in reduced costs to their customers. They were able to offer zero trading. Zero trading fees greatly helps future growth in a portfolio by eliminating ongoing fees putting more money back in your pocket. Another feature I absolutely love about the new platforms is the ability to buy fractional shares. I want to spend some time explaining why this second feature can present an early investor with quite an advantage.

Buying whole shares of stock or fractional shares. Why does it matter? Why is it a big deal? Let's say the average investor wants to invest in common names like Netflix, Amazon, and Apple. Their average stock prices range from 200-2200. For example, if Charlie and Larry (our two characters) wanted to buy at least 1 share of each stock, it may take an entire year to purchase one share. This doesn't fit any early investor's ability to scale into the investment strategy I'm recommending. It doesn't allow them to gradually learn, gain confidence, and put in affordable increments using the dollar cost averaging investing model. In a few chapters, we'll meet Joe the Farmer, who only wants to invest $50 monthly because that's what's affordable to him. If you are closer to Joe the Farmer, then having the ability to purchase $50 monthly, creates that unique opportunity with buying fractional shares. That's why it's so important. It promotes those three things: learning, confidence, and affordability.

With all that said, my preferences and recommendation on choosing the right brokerage account has changed as well. All the below information is as of June 2020 in case anything has changed since the date of publishing. Here's my recommendation with scorecard and commentary below:

Brokerage Account	$0 stock trading fees	Dollar based / fractional share purchases	Robust learning tools	Sign-on bonus	Managed accounts / automation
Fidelity	Yes	Yes	Yes	No	Yes
TD Ameritrade	Yes	No	Yes	Yes	Yes
Robinhood	Yes	Yes	No	No	Yes

Ally Invest	Yes	No	No	Yes	Yes
ACORNs	Yes	No	No	No	Yes

- <u>Fidelity</u> – Trades are $0 per trade for stocks and ETFs, they offer fractional share purchases (with the mobile app), education is robust with a research platform, and they offer several education webinars weekly/monthly among other features

- <u>TD Ameritrade</u> - Trades are $0 per trade for stocks and ETFs. They do not offer fractional share purchases and their educational platform is solid. As of June 2020, they do offer sign-up bonuses with qualifying deposits

- <u>Robinhood</u> – Trades are $0 per trade for stocks and ETFs, they offer fractional share purchases. One glaring item is lack of education (lots of FAQs, but a limited learning platform).

- <u>Ally Bank Invest</u> – Trades are $0 per trade, does not offer fractional share purchases, offers a bonus for sign-up with qualifying deposits, but like Robinhood lacks a true learning platform.

- <u>ACORNs</u> – Not a brokerage account, but an interesting investment option. Company allows consumers to invest spare change into mock portfolios. Good starting choice for brand new investor to get comfortable before switching to brokerage.

My recommendation is Fidelity due to two major advantages that Fidelity offers and others do not. The fractional share purchase option and robust learning environment. Those two differentiating factors are highly valuable for investors of any experience level because of the flexibility and ongoing learning needed to adjust to market conditions. Let's spend a bit more time going over these two options in depth and why they are important variables.

The dollar based or fractional share purchase option is a substantial advantage in building a portfolio of stocks and ETFs in today's marketplace. I mentioned a few paragraphs ago, fractional shares purchase option promotes learning, confidence, and affordability. I want to break this down further because it's that important of a topic. In the early stages of investing, learning about companies of interest, investing in them, and being an owner of the company can help drive long term investment interest. Here's an example of a new investor, Landon.

Landon just had two significant birthdays, at 18 and 21, and has grown up only knowing the world of Amazon, its amazing service platform to order anything, and the lightning speed of delivery to get his stuff quickly. He's also in a test zone that is using drone delivery at times. Now, let's say Landon believes in the business model of Amazon and thinks drone delivery will accelerate over the next decade. If Landon wants to invest in the drone technology (Textron for example, TXT) and Amazon (AMZN) with only $1,000, he'll likely be disappointed in trying to invest in Amazon with a share price of $2,000+ as of June, 2020. Now, by using the Fidelity mobile platform, he can buy fractional shares of Amazon for whatever dollar amount he can afford vs. waiting to purchase 1 share for $2,000+. Fractional shares offer the ability to invest in companies like Amazon, regardless of the stock price, and keeps his interest in the company and business model.

Fast forward to a five years later, let's say drones continue to be a major piece of distribution for Amazon and other distributors. Demand increases and as a result, drone stocks increase in value as well. This will naturally increase the value of Landon's portfolio, which in turn increases his confidence in long term investing. *The principle of long term investing, is a core fundamental this book was built on*. For Landon to begin invest in his own interests with a small initial deposit, Landon had to use the fractional share purchase option. Using fractional share investing is absolutely needed when entering into the marketplace without access to lots of initial capital.

The last important factor to why the fractional share purchase option is really important is affordability. To begin building a portfolio, without lots of available capital, investors like Landon need an affordable option like purchasing fractional shares. Let's say Landon is only starting with $500 to start building his portfolio. Being able to purchase the stock he likes, regardless of the share price and deep pockets, makes affordability an essential attribute. Affordability allows allocating out an initial investment like $500 to multiple months or multiple investments possible. It's also called scaling into investments or dollar cost averaging, as an investment style.

Since we've covered why using fractional share purchases is so important and why it makes Fidelity platform a winner, I'd like to talk through the other important reason. Fidelity's robust learning center that can help push dedicated investors to new levels with their extensive ongoing content. There's so much helpful information on the Fidelity platform to explore, but I want to focus on a few areas I find super helpful when it comes to research.

- Educational webinars – Fidelity puts on reoccurring webinars on a weekly basis that range from topics of Investing 101, Market Insights (what's going on in the market), Technical Analysis education, to Portfolio Management. The experts and frequency breathe relevance into ongoing investment education.

- Investment research– Fidelity has an excellent resource center that I use frequently for stock and ETF research that includes analyst recommendations, fundamental and technical analysis, and plenty of research reports that dive even further.

- New Ideas / Stock Screener – Just like most companies, Fidelity offers stock screeners to find new ideas. A stock screener is just like it sounds. It provides a function that can be used to screen through 100s or 1000s of stocks based on requirements set by the user. A new feature I'd like to call out Fidelity recently introduced is called Themes. <u>Themes</u> consist of ideas like Data Services, Artificial Intelligence, and Big Data to look at themes of stocks. I attached a screenshot below to show how it looks.

- <u>Trading & Investing</u> – These are coaching sessions and learning courses to further understand investment strategy, different types of analysis, and several other useful materials in the world of investing. The best part of these courses is they start at beginner and gradually get tougher to higher levels.

- <u>Personal Finance</u> – This is the how and why of investing. How to plan for retirement, how to plan for college, and even areas like estate planning among others. For things I haven't covered in this book to why investing matters can be found in this section.

Fidelity's Theme Investing

Themes offer another way to start your stock research process. These themes have been identified as areas that may be of interest to our customers and have not been selected based on their investment potential. Companies within themes have varying levels of exposure to the theme, ranging from research and development to generating revenue. Themes include companies that vary in size and type, including growth stocks, which are subject to certain risks and may not be appropriate for all investors. Themes are provided by independent companies not affiliated with Fidelity and the views and values reflected therein may not be reflective of Fidelity's views. More about risks.

This wraps up choosing a brokerage account to build a portfolio in the wonderful world of investing. I hope it's obvious my preferred option is Fidelity. There are other options that offer good services, but I tried to lay out why the Fidelity platform is a better option. Just in case you are wondering, No, I don't get paid by Fidelity to endorse their product. I've just used other platforms and based on my research and personal experience, feel it's much better than other providers.

One more of point of emphasis before moving forward is dividends. Dividends are distributions from the company in the form of a check or reinvest back into the stock. The Board of Directors decides and declares what dividends will be paid to the common shareholders. Dividends are usually paid quarterly and occur on a per share basis. For example, if a company's Board declared a dividend of 12 cents per share, it would equal $0.12 for every share owned. If owning 100 shares, it receives $12 in a dividend payment, giving the option to reinvest it as stock or be paid out in cash. Occasionally, companies will issue stock dividends instead of a cash dividend. The biggest difference in a stock dividend is that the stock dividends are not taxed until sold, whereas cash dividends are taxed within the calendar tax year they are received.

Chapter Six

THE ACTUAL NUMBER NEEDED TO REACH RETIREMENT

O nce retirement starts to get closer to reality, most people begin to plan for how much they will need to maintain a comfortable lifestyle. Do people know how much money should be saved annually to have the type of retirement people picture in their minds? Even if it's not clear the exact amount being saved for, it's OK. Just don't let that thought linger forever without a plan. My goal is for this section to start the idea by asking some questions to further understand the type of retirement you dream about to effectively plan for it.

Typically, retirement planning starts with establishing some goals and then deciding what wants, needs, and desires you are looking to fulfill. Identifying what type of monthly income is needed is a great starting point. It helps to understand how much will be needed to draw from a portfolio in highly anticipated retirement years. Let's start that process right here now. What are some of the dreams (even long stretching ones) you want to do or accomplish after leaving the traditional workforce?

- Want to travel?
- Where are those destinations?
  - Plan on having an annual vacation budget? If so, how much?
  - What types of things do you want do on vacation?
    - Scuba dive?
    - Travel to rain forests and zip line?
    - Weekly massages?
    - Hang gliding or exploring volcanoes?
    - Go shopping in famous stores in Paris?
    - Stay at expensive resorts or go backpacking?
- What about buvying a vacation property? If so where?
  - In Florida? Specifically in Key West? Orlando? Sarasota? Boca Raton?
  - Hawaii? Which island?

○ The Mountains? Possibly Colorado or Salt Lake City, Utah?

○ Jamaica?

○ Thailand?

• Any interest in teaching or writing a novel?

• Any interest in buying a boat or motorcycle?

• Learn something new and take classes?

• What about charity or volunteer work?

• Are there any events to possibly train to do, like a marathon?

• How much is the current mortgage payment and also owed on the mortgage?

Any of these questions should start some thoughts about the type of property, type of activities, or type of anything part of the retirement future. The of exercise is to point out that some things cost money and some do not. The monetary activities vary in price depending on where, when, and the extent of it. The wide-ranging ideas should spark some thinking about retirement plans and how to plan a potential budget for that anticipated time. This planning process should result to have an annual or monthly number about how much money it will take to retire and live those dreams. Don't forget about the essential costs that need to be covered as well. These are basic living expenses (mortgage), insurance, food, and the bare necessities in life.

To achieve these goals, let's start with a strategy to set the right course. There are options available to help get there like a 401K plan, Individual Retirement Account (IRA), or a Roth IRA account. These are retirement accounts that grow tax-deferred (tax-free) until the mandatory retirement age where withdrawals are required later in life. I cover these options in more detail later in the book in "Account Types and Setting Them Up" section in Chapter 13.

The personal investment strategy that each person chooses should change over time. Specific events happen all the time in life that can increase or decrease expenses like marriages, children, job moves, or even tragedies and accidents. The takeaway here is the plan is to adjust the plan when necessary, but having a strategy to get back on plan.

The last place most folks want to be is working some meaningless retail part-time job later in their life as a door greeter or cashier. Jobs like these serve as nothing more than just necessary income due to poor planning. I'm not talking about doing something people actually want to do, such as helping a nursery grow flowers or writing part-time. I'm referencing jobs like handing out flyers for a store in the mall or folding clothes at GAP.

Most people are looking to maintain a comfortable retirement without running out of money by planning accordingly. There is an actual formula to calculate how much you should be saving. Remember I mentioned Fidelity, right? On their website (www. fidelity.com), there are fantastic FREE retirement calculators that take into account several factors to provide a realistic view of what's needed. Look through the several calculators that work best for your interest and goals. All the information can be found on Fidelity's site here and look through the calculators. Some of these things are already known, and there's a few items that will either have to be projections or best guesstimates.

- Current Age – known
- What age planning on retiring – guesstimate
- Amount currently in retirement savings – known
- Current annual salary – known

- Percentage contributed currently to 401K – known
    - Company match – known
- Average Return – requires research

All of this information can be found on the site mentioned above. Most importantly, all the information is **FREE** and easily accessible. One huge benefit of going through this exercise is that it tells the amount that can be withdrawn annually (similar to an annual salary) to plan accordingly without running out of money. It's a great exercise to provide guidance of how much investing and saving is needed to prepare for the life desired. It's not easy at first and does take some practice. Go ahead and give it a try.

Keep one last thing in mind before we move forward: these retirement calculators only take into account these variables mentioned. Keep in mind my contributing 1-2% more how that would impact the retirement plan? What if there are separate investments (a rental property or retail investments that can be converted into retirement) that produce income regularly? Those will propel the retirement goals even faster towards and past these financial expectations. All of this information should prompt thinking to get a plan of action to achieve a comfortable retirement. That's the end goal.

THE FORMULA

If by chance the financial calculators aren't what you are looking for (especially for retail investments), don't worry there are other ways. Microsoft has a very easy-to-use formula without being Excel savvy. I can show you how to calculate how much a future value can turn into regardless of the financial goal. The formula is called FV, or Future Value. Within the formula, there are specific values needed. To put these ideas into practice, let's try out actual examples below.

- Rate = Annual rate of return. For example, what is the annual rate of return the investment is expected to generate? If this is not known, use 8% as a conservative estimate. It's wise to use monthly so divide by 12.

- Nper = total number of payments during the investment period, or the number of payments expected to make towards the goal. For example, if 5 years of payments are expected monthly, then 60 is the answer (5 x 12).

- Pmt = The payment made each period that will not change over the investment period. For example, if 60 payments of $100 each time are expected, then use 100. This is very helpful for a 401k plan to see what the monthly contributions will add up to.

- PV = Present value or the starting amount. This could be 0 or an amount. For example, rather than making monthly payments, if starting with $10,000, then plug in 10,000 as the PV to start.

- Type = Timing of payment. This only matters if the investment is made at the beginning or end of the cycle. Basically, it means is the monthly investment at the beginning of the month or the end of the month. Use 1 for the beginning and 0 for the end.

Good, now that we've gone through the elements, let's use the formula.

- In any cell, type in =FV (rate, number of payments, payment, present value, use 0 for type)

Note – The formula will produce a negative number using this because it must read the future value (FV) and present value (PV) differently.

REAL EXAMPLES USING THESE CALCULATIONS

Mark Saver wants to put together a strategy to purchase a new home for his family. He has **$10,000** currently to invest, expects to earn a ROI of **11%**, and will invest **$150 a month** for **three years** for a down payment on a house. How much will Mark end up with? Let's calculate it by using Microsoft Excel training from above. Here's what the formula looks like =FV (.11/12, 36, 150, 10000, 0) = $20,252.25. Imagine if Mark can wait one more year at the same rate for the down payment. The down payment goes up to $24,489.40. Let's say Mark uses the same formula, but is able to contribute $250 per month over three years. The amount goes to $24,494.57. Almost another year with just another $100 per month in savings can make a huge difference towards his goal of saving enough for a home purchase. This can be figured out by simply interchanging the variables.

Sarah Supersaver is a typical single working mother. She has a regular job and is in charge of taking care of her two kids. Due to her uncle's passing, she just inherited $50,000 and won't retire for at least another 20 years. Like most folks, she currently budgets monthly and doesn't have much left over because of her kids and monthly expenses. Because of this, Sarah doesn't plan to contribute anything more to the lump sum. In addition to not contributing towards the money, she has already committed not to touch the $50,000 unless there is an absolute emergency. Sarah decides to invest the money based on her father's advice in an low risk ETF, and estimates an average rate of return of 10%. What will the $50,000 add up to in 20 years? =FV (.10, 20, 0, 50000, 0) = $336,375. She will have over $300,000 available to her if she stays to her plan and not touch the money for at least 20 years by allowing it to grow. Add another 10 years and it balloons to $872,470.11. Now, we are talking about a substantial amount to use for retirement and her kids!

Mike "Monthly" Mathis is our next example. Mike just got out of college and really doesn't make a lot of money. Mike has a specific advantage because he still lives at home with his parents and doesn't have to contribute to rent because he is paying off student loans. During Mike's college studies, he took a class on Investment Analysis. He remembered about the power of compound interest and knew even small amounts can add up over time. Mike decides to contribute $50 monthly to a stable investment for the next 4 years. Also, Mike just got a signing bonus of $1,500 at his new job, and will use $300 of it immediately towards his growing portfolio. He estimates a modest 7% ROI because the investment he chose is lower in risk. What does Mike's portfolio look like with low monthly investments after 4 years and the initial $300? =FV (.07/12, 48, 50, 300, 0) = $3,157. The amount jumps to $3,157. After only three years, Mike has saved over $3,000. If he continues with $50 monthly and leaves the rest to grow for at least 10 years, at the same ROI rate of 7%, the $3000 will grow into over $15,000.

Debbie "The Shopper" Debt Davis has a very expensive habit that takes most of her paycheck. It's called shoes and the mall. Over the last two years, Debbie has racked up significant credit card debt due to her overwhelming love for shoes. Debbie has a total of $12,000 in credit card debt with a high interest rate of 15.99% APR. Debbie Debt Davis visited her local bank branch and consolidated the debt for a lower rate of 1.99% over 18 months. Debbie must figure out how much she needs to pay to become debt free. Instead of paying down the debt directly at $677.21 per month, Debbie can wait the 18 months and put that money towards an investment to pay it off at once. Debbie figures she can earn at least 10% on investments and keep the difference. The new formula is called the Payment Formula and has all the same elements of FV, but in a different order. It's =PMT(rate, number of payments, present value, future value, and type). =PMT (.10/12, 18, 0, 12000, 0) = $620.68. To satisfy the $12,000, she will invest the money and pay off the debt all at once instead of monthly payments to the bank.

Do any of these examples seem to reflect your current lifestyle? The point of each of these examples is to provide real life examples of events that happen, and understand how to apply the principals of using compound interest in financial situations. The other key takeaway is to clearly identify how to put an investment plan into action to achieve long term goals. Paying yourself in a different account will provide the opportunity to grow income at a higher rate of return.

Feel free to use these formulas in Microsoft Excel or with a financial calculator when purchasing a new car as well. This is how the finance guys will calculate monthly car payments and try to get the best deal for them. Knowing some of this information in advance instead of just "taking their word for it", will help a lot with the negotiations to be much better off. Now that we know how to calculate what the nest egg should shape into, let's go ahead and move into how investments can be taxed as an overview when it comes to strategy with money.

Chapter Seven

TAXES: HOW INVESTING
IMPACTS TAXES

Before I start, I'd like to note this is not a book on taxes. They have an impact on investments. For that reason, I wanted to at least cover taxes at a high level since all investing strategies will have some type of tax implications. With that said, let's get to it. Whenever selling a stock (publicly traded company) from a brokerage account, there will be some taxes to pay on gains or losses to claim depending on how long the stock was owned. There are strategies regarding investing and how it will impact personal income taxes. Before we jump into this, let's discuss briefly how this was handled prior to 2012 with cost basis regulations. The cost basis is the price of the security that was initially paid for when the stock purchase was made.

Prior to 2012, legislators had been making the case for years that the U.S. Government wasn't getting their fair share of tax proceeds from capital gains due to cost basis. Cost basis can be confusing all by itself depending on how on investment cadence in the stock market. For example, by using an investment strategy of dollar cost averaging by investing in the same stock many times a year, that could be multiple tax lots over several times a year over several years. Throw in potential dividends, stock splits, reverse stock splits, or mergers, and it can really get confusing rather quickly.

I must admit, I get confused by it as well, and that's why I have a good accountant to help me with all the tax questions. Legislators didn't exactly come out and say it, but the underlying notion was that people were cheating on the original cost basis. When an individual investor sold a stock position, only the sale proceeds was reported to the IRS, not the cost basis. This left a reporting gap in how much gain or loss was attributed to the investment and the stock owner. The onus was always on the individual to correctly report the correct cost basis.

Just by outlining the above scenarios, investors can quickly see how the cost basis process can be very confusing in general. Most people probably weren't trying to skirt the taxes, but they just got perplexed within the process itself and tried the best they could. Fast forward to 2012, and Congress passed cost basis legislation that would require financial institutions to report the capital gains and cost basis directly to the IRS. This alleviates the issue from individuals tracking it themselves anymore. This is both good and bad.

The legislation was split up among stocks, bonds, and different plan types to allow companies to catch up to the new requirements. This action was later amended to be spread out over a few years because of the complexity of implementing technology solutions to their existing platforms. Companies were required to spend millions of dollars to implement the technology to track everything and accurately report to the IRS.

The fact that companies are spending high dollar amounts should matter, but should it? Companies might eventually look to pass that cost along to the brokerage houses and end investors in some form, so yes, it should be a concern. This brings us up to speed on today's financial environment. The below sections should make it easier to understand how investments will impact taxes. When a stock is sold, there could be tax consequences caused by gaining or losing money. Taxes are broken down into Short Term and Long Term Capital Gains or Losses.

SHORT TERM GAINS/LOSSES

Short term gains and losses are characterized as a market sale that occurs less than one calendar year. Basically, if a marketable security (for example - stock, bond, etc.) is sold less than 365 days after purchase, it's subject to being taxed at a short term gain at the individual's tax bracket level. For example, if the investor has the 28% tax bracket, the short term gains will be taxed at a 28% rate. Only the profits are taxed, not the entire position or principal amount.

Here's an example to explain this process in more detail. Larry (remember him) bought 10 shares of Stock A in January 2014 for $100 per share. Six months later in July 2014, the stock price rose to $140 per share. Larry wanted to cash out his profit of $400 ($1,400 - $1,000) to lock in the increase in stock price. Since the realized gains (sale on record) were sold in less than 12 months, Larry's profit was taxed at the short term gains tax level. Remember, only the gain of $400 will be taxed, not the entire position of $1400. See below:

- Stock A bought (10 shares) for $1,000 in **January 2014**
- Stock A sold for $1,400 in **July 2014**
- Cost basis is $1,000, and $1,400 is reported to the IRS,
    - This results in $400 taxable gain @28% taxes = $400 x.28 = $112
    - Larry owes $112 on his taxes to the IRS

On the opposite end of short term gains are short term losses. These losses are handled just like long term losses (this will be addressed on the next page). The losses can be helpful as a strategy in offsetting gains with another stock position to avoid paying taxes on a specific gain. Take the example above where the investor Larry sold Stock A and recorded $400 in gains. If at any time during the same tax year Larry also sold Stock B for a loss of $300, the realized gain/loss would offset, and the investor would only be required to pay taxes on $100 gain ($400-$300). This gain would then come out to only $28 ($100 gain x .28) since Larry was in the 28% tax bracket.

This type of example is why many investors usually look to sell positions that have a negative return towards the end of the year. This is used to lower the tax burden from potential gains realized or to offset dividends that will be taxed (yes dividends are taxed). If selling a stock specifically for the tax break and plan on re-buying the position, there's a specific rule to keep the investment clear of negating the tax loss called the **Wash Rule.** I'll explain in more detail below.

> ➤ **One IMPORTANT NOTE** – If selling a stock for a loss (as described above to gain a tax benefit) and intend to buy the stock back at any time, it's a rule the investor must wait 30 calendar days according to the Wash Rule. **The Wash Rule** sale window spans 61 days (30 days before the sale, the sale date, and the 30 days after the sale). The IRS created the Wash Rule intending to impose regulation on tax deductions to claim a loss on taxes. This was accomplished by requiring any investor to wait the full 30 calendar days following a sale to purchase the same stock position again. If the Wash Rule is violated, it is illegal and will result in the benefit of a loss being negated.

Selling securities to gain a tax benefit and buying them back immediately is illegal according to the Tax Reform Act of 1984.

➤ *Just remember*, **wait at least 30 calendar days to buy the same position to claim the loss for taxes. After 30 full calendar days have passed, go ahead and re-buy the same stock position. This will keep folks out of trouble with the IRS and the tax benefit.**

LONG TERM GAINS / LOSSES

Long term capital gains or losses are defined as an investment owned longer than 12 months and then sold. The law was changed recently on how much capital gains and dividends were taxed. Prior to 2012, the law read that people would pay taxes at a 15% rate for long term capital gains and dividends. The law was recently changed to increase the rate to 20% until the tax laws regarding dividends are revisited in the future. Just like before, let's put this into action by providing an example with short term realized gains, long term gains, and dividends.

SHORT TERM GAINS / LOSSES (THIS WAS FROM THE PREVIOUS EXAMPLE)

- Stock A is bought for $1,000 on **January 21, 2014**

- Stock A is sold for $1,200 on **July 31, 2014**

- Cost Basis is $1,000, and $1,200 is reported to the IRS

  ○ This results in $200 tax gain @28% taxes = $200 x .20 = $56

  ○ The investor owes $56 in taxes

LONG TERM GAINS / LOSSES (THIS IS THE NEW EXAMPLE)

- Stock A is bought for $1,000 on **January 21, 2013**

- Stock A is sold for $1,200 on **January 31, 2014**

- Cost Basis is $1,000, and $1,200 is reported to the IRS

  ○ This results in $200 tax gain @20% taxes = $200 x .20 = $40

  ○ The investor owes $40 in taxes

Same example using **Dividends** now -

- An investor owns 200 shares of Stock A in 2014 and earns $25 in dividends for the year
- The investor is taxed on the $25 in dividends
- The tax rate is 20%, resulting in $5 owed
  - The investor owes $5 in taxes

Again, long term losses are treated in the same manner as short term losses. They can be used to offset gains in a calendar year to reduce the potential tax burden. The sales must be completed prior to December 31 to use it for tax purposes. For example, if the sale of long term Stock A results in a $1000 gain towards the end of the year along with $40 in dividends, and long term Stock B's sale can result in a $500 long term loss, then the net is a $540 gain for which taxes are owed. The biggest difference now is that since these are long term gains, the gains are taxed at the 20% level (the current long terms gain rate) along with the dividends at the same rate.

There's one more area regarding capital losses that's important for long term investors (which I want everyone to become) that I need to address. Capital losses are netted against gains. If losses exceed gains, an investor may use up to $3,000 to deduct from ordinary income during that tax year. **If losses exceed $3,000, the**

losses may be carried forward to the next tax year. For example, if by chance there's $4,000 of stock losses, the $3,000 can be applied in the current year and carry forward $1,000 in the following year against taxable income. Visually, let's go through the example:

- In 2014, Larry owes $900 in personal income taxes
- In 2014, Larry has a portfolio loss of $5,000
- The $900 is covered up by the loss of $5,000 (leaving $4,100 in losses)
- Larry can take up to $3,000 in stock losses towards personal income tax that year
- In 2015, Larry can carry the $1,100 loss forward towards income or stock gains to offset and of course PAY LESS TAXES

That should clear things up from an overview, give some structure to stocks from a broad taxes perspective, and provide some high level understanding. Always remember, regardless of the result, there is always a strategy that can be used to benefit (and sometimes boost) the investor. If there's specific questions regarding taxes and how investing can potentially impact them, I would advise to speak with an accountant or check this section in Fidelity.com on taxes.

BONDS

Bonds are a fixed income investment product and will be essential to a balanced portfolio as people at age. Bonds come in handy when investors have less working power (closer to retirement) and need to start reducing risk in their portfolios. Bonds are lower risk products that help retain the principal and serve as a fixed income financial product. This is a necessary product as retirement nears and people begin to draw against their portfolio. Bonds are issued by companies and governments to borrow money for capital projects. Most investors buy bonds with a par value of $1,000 and expect to receive $1,000 when the bond reaches maturity along with coupon payments. Bonds are made up of the following elements:

- Par Value (also called principal or face value) – Face value or $1,000 (most are sold at Par)
- Maturity Date (also called Due Date) – Date for return and last interest payment due

- Interest Rate (also called the Nominal Yield) – This is the coupon rate (interest payment) and yield earned, stated annually, paid semi-annually

- Discount / Premium – If the price is above or below par ($1,000)

Interest payments and bond prices are stated as percentages of par -

- 1% or 1 point for a bond = $10 ($1,000 x.01)
- ¼ of a point for a bond = $2.50 ($1,000 x .0025)

For example, if Mike Jones owns a 6% bond, which means he receives $60.00 in interest spread out over the length of the loan. He bought the bond for 94 ½ for the bond or $945.00 ($1,000 x .945). That means the bond sold at a discount since it was sold under par ($1,000). To get further information on real bond quotes and to see how bonds are priced out, check out www.Bloomberg.com.

Bonds have an inverse relationship to interest rates, as the interest rate changes, the bond price moves in the opposite direction. This means there are more favorable times to buy bonds, such as when interest rates rise. Interest rates have been historically low since 2014, once they begin to rise, money will likely start to move into bond investments. Here's an easy table to look at to determine if the bond is selling a discount or a premium. Since interest rates change, their inverse relationship affects bond prices like this:

	Market Rate	Coupon on Bond	Market Price
Sold			
When Issued	7%	7%	Par ($1,000)
After Issued	9%	7%	Discount
Even later after Issued	5%	7%	Premium

This should provide a high level of understanding about how bonds work and some of the advantages associated with them for fixed income investors. There is a specific circumstance that may arise that could result in the bond being called by the issuer (company or government) earlier than maturity. This means the bond issuer will pay the bond holder off earlier than expected. This is referred to as call feature, which allows the issuer to redeem the bonds prior to maturity. Similar to the option to refinance a house if interest rates fall, issuers can do the same exact thing and must pay a premium to offer the call feature.

Bond issuers will allow them to redeem the bonds before they are due to mature. If a company could do this and it was stated in the contract, why would they offer this and why would an investor accept the offer? The reasons or factors that make callable bonds attractive are:

- Higher Yield – bonds will be selling at a lower price
- Call Protection – An investor is protected for a specific length of time during which a bond cannot be redeemed, alleviating any surprises
- Call Premium – Issuers must pay the investor a higher premium for redeeming the bonds early

To conduct business, corporations raise money by issuing stocks and bonds. The benefit for the corporation of issuing bonds instead of stock, is borrowing the money over the long term from investors with a set return in the form of interest. A corporation must pay interest on bonds prior to any funds in dividends to both common and preferred shareholders. Buying bonds provides a much lower risk than if the investor buys the common stock in the same company, but doesn't provide the same type of potential in regards of return on investment. Similarly, governments do the same thing.

Local and state Governments issue bonds when they need to raise money to pay for projects like roads, highways, and schools. There is a distinct difference though when comparing company issued, government issued and municipal issued bonds. Municipal bonds have specific exemptions depending on several factors meaning this could be part of a fixed income portfolio and tax strategy if needed. The interest received is exempt from Federal tax, but could be subject to state and local taxes depending on residence. Although interest is exempt from taxes, capital gains are taxable. Depending on the bond, they have different tax exemptions.

TAX EXAMPLES – HOW TO CALCULATE BOND ROI AFTER TAXES

Below I'll explain how to understand the true rate of return when considering taxes in the equation. The first example is a tax free rate (most like a municipal bond) and the second example is a taxable rate (most likely a corporate bond).

TAX FREE RATE

Mr. Smith is earning 5.6% interest on a tax free municipal bond and is in the 35% tax bracket. What is the equivalent in taxable income? 5.6 / (1-.35) = 8.6%

TAX RATE

Mrs. Smith purchased a 7.5% corporate bond and is in the 35% tax bracket. What amount will Mrs. Smith keep after taxes? 7.5% x (1 − .35) = 4.88%

One last note on taxes: Here is a breakdown chart that I use and find helpful when it comes to which entity's bond is subject to federal or state taxes:

	Subject to Taxes	
Source	Federal?	State?
Corporate Bonds	Yes	Yes
Municipal Bonds	No	Maybe
US Treasury Bills	Yes	No
Debt of Territories	No	No

As investors age and can no longer tolerate risk, bonds provide a good alternative to stocks because of their fixed income characteristics.

Chapter Eight

Forming an Investment Plan & Strategy

I'd like to begin to tie everything we learned thus far together, when it comes to creating an investment strategy and plan. Investors should have some type of investment plan versus just figuring it along the way. There are several strategies for stock market investing. Variables we'll need to review along the way are how many positions to hold, allocation to each position, how much should to have in cash, and when to shift the portfolio into lower risk or fixed income? Each answer prompts the plan and direction of the future strategy. I'm going to begin to provide some recommendations in the coming pages to an investing strategy.

To get started, let's begin with a bunch of basic questions with easy accessible answers. The questions are meant to help to intersect personal finance with developing an investment strategy and how to view investing. It's really important because the answers will provide insight to where expense management can translate into investing:

- How often is the mortgage payment paid? Monthly or bi-weekly?
- What about car payment & insurance payments?
- Are these items paid on a specific day each month?
- What about the cell phone bill?
- Are these paid monthly, quarterly, or annually?
- What about the other bills? (cable bill, power bill, water bill)?
- Are all of the above bills paid prior to the deadline or on time?

Now, I'd like to use the same logic and point out a psychological difference that we discussed earlier in the book regarding how well you track personal payments.

- How often do you pay yourself? Monthly? Quarterly? Do you ever pay yourself?

These questions will help connect personal finance, spending habits, and transition to forming an investment plan. Is there a difference between paying someone else to provide a service monthly and paying yourself? Between monthly bills, monthly income, and the discretionary income (the leftovers), how much should be contributed to the investment strategy.

Can you afford to pay yourself at least $50 per month or even as high as $1,000 per month? What does it mean for the annual budget? Start to understand the monthly budget and expenses versus how much can be committed to routinely paying yourself. A payment to yourself should have the same weight and importance of paying a bill, creditor, or even a service (or shoes for the shoe lovers!). Fear of getting charged late fees, having bad credit, and getting assessed interest charges are all tools companies use to deter late payments. Companies that provide a service expect to get paid on time (with the exception of credit cards that earn extra income from interest charges). Use that same discipline in paying yourself often and on time.

MONTHLY INVESTMENTS

One of the best ways to pay yourself is to treat it like any other bill, and pay yourself monthly. This goes into the psychology of investing and changing current behavior by routinely paying yourself in a DIFFERENT ACCOUNT. It *absolutely must be a separate account* other than a savings or checking account to break the traditional human psychology. Breaking that habit with human psychology will deter keeping extra cash sitting in an account without earning any significant interest. This type of monthly investing strategy using the same amount is called dollar cost averaging.

Let use a brief story about Joe the Farmer that helps to further illustrate the point. Joe the Farmer has $50 to buy cows each month and has that exact amount set aside to do so. Let's say the price of cows fluctuates from month to month and Joe always buys $50 worth, if he can't afford the entire cow, they give him credit towards the purchase of another cow in the following month. He commits to trying this practice for the following year. His purchases look like this -

- January – Cow Price $22.50 – Joe buys 2.22 cows ($50/22.50)

- February – Cow Price $21.50 – Joe buys 2.33 cows

- March – Cow Price $24.00 – Joe buys 2.08 cows

- April – Cow Price $25.00 – Joe buys 2 cows

- May – Cow Price $24.00 – Joe buys 2.08 cows

- June – Cow Price $23.50 – Joe buys 2.13 cows

- July – Cow Price $22.50 – Joe buys 2.22 cows

- August – Cow Price $19.50 – Joe buys 2.56 cows

- September – Cow Price $17.50 – Joe buys 2.86 cows

- October – Cow Price $22.50 – Joe buys 2.22 cows

- November – Cow Price - $25.00 - Joe buys 2 cows

- December – Cow Price - $26.00 – Joe buys 1.92 cows

- Total cows bought for the year – 26.62 – valued at $692.12 for the year

- Total money spent - $600.00

- A valuation profit of $92.12 or 15.3%

Joe the farmer consistently bought cows all year long at $50 a month, regardless of the price because this was his strategy for his farm. At the end of the year, if he sold all his cows at the current rate, he would realize a gain of 15.3%. This is exactly how a dollar cost strategy works with an investment portfolio today. Now, go ahead and substitute cows with stocks or ETFs (remember this is an Exchange Traded Fund, which is a basket of stocks). This strategy works just like it did for Joe the Farmer when replacing the cows. Dollar cost averaging works by investing an equal amount of money regularly during a specified period. Just like the Joe the Farmer example, the fractional shares (instead of fractional cows) are also purchased into the investment account that will earn equity too. Using Fidelity's fractional purchase ability, this strategy is possible to purchase any investment of choice.

I highly recommend this strategy because it relates to the exact same type of monthly budgeting that the majority of the population currently practices. Think about it, people are constantly managing a monthly budget and have a good idea of how much is generally left over with a spending plan (remember the spending plan?). Take the initiative and start paying yourself with those funds. I'm not talking about leaving it in a savings account passively, I'm saying actually remove the money to another account. I started using this strategy when I was in college at a mere $50 a month just like Joe the farmer and have since increased it with salary adjustments, life changes and good saving habits. Start practicing this and don't even bother to look at it for at least a few months. It may even be a surprise with the results that are possible. Remember the example of Mike "Monthly" Mathis and his ability to save over $3,000 in three short years? Mike saved the money.

Now that I've laid down a monthly investment strategy of how to invest, let's look at which investment approach works best. I've read several other investment books and the authors are consistent with recommending the ideal portfolio of 15-20 stocks to help diversify risk and investment classes. I'm going to follow the same logic. I'll mix some of that and some other concepts that will help build a strong portfolio without frequent updates. Let's be honest, the majority of the population works full-time jobs and doesn't have the time to research or monitor their portfolio in the way that they would really like. I want to introduce a portfolio type that easy to setup and check it once every three months. As I move forward, I'll use the analogy of building a house, because in many ways building a house is the same process of building (and maintaining) a strong portfolio. Here's how to do it:

THE FORT

Everything starts with The Fort. What's The Fort? Let's use an analogy to explain. When a construction crew first decides how to build a house, where do they start first? They check the land to make sure the house can sustain itself once constructed on the land. They then move to laying the foundation of the house with brick, rebar (steel), and concrete. It's about the foundation. Before the fun house designs come to the table, the foundation is the first and most significant piece to withstand the test of time, especially high degrees of inclement weather throughout a person's life. The foundation for a house has the same level of importance as The Fort when it comes to setting up the foundation of the portfolio. The Fort will help weather the ups and downs of the stock market by providing the required stability and safety to grow an effective portfolio.

Now, what is The Fort, and what does it consist of? Good question!

- **The Fort** – This will consist of 3-5 Index ETFs that spread across multiple asset classes (Large Cap, Mid-Cap & Small Cap) and multiple styles (Mixed, Value, & Growth). Remember, an ETF acts just like a mutual fund with the biggest difference is fees are dramatically less. An individual mutual fund consists of hundreds of different stocks to spread out the potential risk just like an ETF. By utilizing ETFs, it means the fees are much lower, which in turn keeps more money with the investor vs. the company. An ETF can be purchased just like a stock and it provides flexibility when it comes to buying and selling. The Fort will spread out enough allocation to several stocks, so it will reduce the risk significantly. Not only does it reduce risk, but it reduces the need to constantly watch the portfolio. The ideal percentage allocation to The Fort is between 30-50% of the total portfolio depending on tolerance to risk.

There are literally thousands of ETFs to choose from in today's stock market, so I'll suggest a few to start (they are also covered in "mock portfolios" and more choices in the index). There are three major players when it comes to Mutual Funds in today's economic landscape – Vanguard, T. Rowe Price, and Fidelity. There are hundreds if not thousands more, but these three are some of the top providers when it comes to asset allocation and longevity. Why am I bringing up Mutual Funds in the ETF section? I have done so to explain that these premium mutual funds have been around for quite a long time to demonstrate stability in their brands.

Back in Chapter 6, we spent considerable time discussing the value of using Fidelity as the brokerage account of choice. The have all the options we need, including the ETFs to create The Fort. Fidelity does a great job of mirroring their professionally managed mutual funds as well as the ongoing investment advice through their learning center. For these reasons, I would recommend using their products to build The Fort in the portfolio (and NOT Mutual Funds).

I keep bringing up the pros of ETFs and the cons of Mutual Funds because I really want to drive home the point of which to choose and more importantly why to choose. Outflows (money exiting) of Mutual Funds have begun to speed up in recent years, while inflows of cash are growing ETFs at a record pace. It's a trend that many people are getting behind and I want all investors to be on the right side too. Just remember that ETFs should be part of your portfolio with 30-50% consisting of different ETFs to cover The Fort.

Chapter Nine

PICKING STOCKS

After The Fort is setup and ready for the rest of the surrounding "material", how to select a stock? Pick them at random? Rely on tips or recommendations from others? Ever known or seen someone ask a colleague for advice on 401k allocation? I have. Too often folks in offices ask their cubicle neighbors in their vicinity to help select their 401K plans. I'm sure the closets cube mate is great for helping with projects, but are they really that helpful at selecting stocks and managing someone's retirement savings? What about talk radio? Do radio hosts or TV hosts on news stations talk about stocks all the time? Is it difficult to differentiate who to listen to about what stocks to buy and which to ignore? These are solutions on how NOT to select stocks.

What about internet hot stock tips? What about the guy on Fast Money who screams on television most of the time? (You probably know who I mean). Use this rule of thumb. The general public is the last to receive any inside stock information, as the rumors circulated have already bypassed the company affected and analysts covering the company. So back to question one, how to select a stock? What criteria should be used? There are several ways. I'm going to concentrate on three different ways I'm going to introduce to select potential companies to invest in. The Common Sense Way, the Wall Street Way, and the EFT Breakdown Way.

THE COMMON SENSE WAY

Don't worry, this way isn't as analytical as the professionals on Wall Street, but trust me, it can be just as effective. You're a smart consumer and know other smart consumers. People establish habits and tend to shop, eat, and purchase the same type of goods. Let's go ahead and run through a consumer's typical day (including both life and work) to see what company's products that are used. All products or companies are labeled beforehand and the corresponding symbol follows in ().

John, our typical consumer wakes up, and turns off his Sony (SNE) alarm clock, brushes with his Proctor and Gamble (PG) toothbrush followed by a rinse with Johnson & Johnson (JNJ) Listerine. Oh wait, before that was done, John's Duke Energy (DUK) electricity was running the entire time to power the lights, followed by using the sink with water from Aqua America (WTR). After finishing up in the bathroom and using a few more products from Proctor and Gamble (toilet paper & paper towels), John proceeds to get dressed. After putting on his clothes from Macy's (M), running downstairs to get some Kellogg's (K) Eggo Waffles, he checks his iPhone (AAPL) on Verizon's (VZ) mobile network and WIFI from his Google (GOOG) email account and check Facebook (FB) to see what his friends are up to this weekend. John then decides to concentrate on the day and switches over to his iPad (AAPL) for work emails in Microsoft Outlook (MSFT).

After breakfast, John hops in his Toyota 4Runner SUV (TM) stop for coffee from Starbucks (SBUX) and fills up the tank at Chevron (CVX) gas station. John gets to work, and needs to run out at lunch to PetSmart (PETM) to get dog food for Snoopy and stops at Target (TGT) to grab Diet Coke (KO) for the office party to celebrate his co-worker's birthday pizza party catered by Papa John's (PZZA).

After work, John agrees to meet friends at Bahama Breeze (Darden Restaurants (DRI)) for drinks. During Happy Hour, John's wife texts him and asks him to stop by Costco (COST) to grab extra steaks because the in-laws are coming over for dinner and he won't have enough for everyone. One last stop before heading home. What a day for John.

Whew! That's a lot of companies encountered without realizing. It was right around 20 companies in total for just one day that John used. I didn't even bother to mention several companies that built John's house, manufactured products in his office, or even the stores he shopped for goods during his chaotic day. Knowing that most of these companies are engaged with every day should make John as a consumer feel smarter after daily routine. Consumers like John that shop using the same habits allow businesses like these to remain profitable year in, year out. This could easily be the portfolio.

When companies upgrade their technology or products, consumers keep coming back for more. What new technologies do you love? Want to drive an electric sports car like Tesla (TSLA)?

What about the new iPhone or iPad (AAPL)? The next time a new purchase comes up, find out who makes it and if the demand is similar among close friends. This happens all the time, and sometimes by simple observation. Let's go into this a little further.

This is exactly what I meant by using the common sense model. It just takes effort to stop and observe the companies used on a regular basis. These observations just require attention and effort. Michael Gelb wrote in his book, "Thinking like Leonardo", about Leonardo Da Vinci's curious nature in observing and the development of ideas. One of the concepts centered on refining the senses, especially sight, to enhance experiences. Think about your observations as potential investment ideas. New ideas are constantly coming in the form of advertising regardless of channel (mobile ads, web surfing, streaming services, TV). By increasing the ability of sensing with products, it will improve business sense to identify potential investments. Let's talk about more investment ideas.

Smartphones appear to be the norm these days, right? Regardless of the type of phone (most are Apple (AAPL) or Samsung) the two world leaders in smartphones, there's a way to invest in the technology that powers them. Qualcomm (QCOM) is one of them. They provide technology solutions to both companies. There's also semi-conductors in the phone (parts that make the phone functional). A company like Skyworks (SWKS) that powers the WIFI connection. Keep in mind, these are just ideas to give an example to dig further. If you have zero interest (like the majority of the public) in researching which companies will outperform others, I'd recommend using the Common Sense Way.

Now that we've the Common Sense Way to investing, let's discuss the Wall Street Way to investments. This includes using a stock screener, reading specific ratios, and scrutinizing investments in more detail the company behind the stock. It requires a bit more analysis and research, but when finding a winning stock in the bunch, trust me, it's worth it.

Side Story #1 - Think of a revolutionary product. One of my first experiences was with the iPod. I remember early on when the iPod just came out. I had an Intel (INTC) MP3 player at the time and a friend of mine had just bought the iPod. I observed the simplicity of the iPod and compared it to my Intel MP3 player. It was a much better product. Within the next 3-6 months, I slowly saw all of my friends had iPods and it wasn't long until I had one too. At the time, Apple's stock was trading *around $10 per share. At that very moment, I should have recognized that Apple was onto something, a massive disruption to the industry. This meant the iPod was exploding onto the scene, and it was ultimately the end of the Walkman and portable CD player. We as consumers knew it was a beautiful game changing product when it arrived. The same thing happened years later with the iPhone. The iPhone would go on as one of the greatest technology enhancements in history. Those are the moments to look out for when it comes to products in your life and capitalize on the potential as it relates to the common marketplace. Take that knowledge and understand how to make a smart investment.*

THE WALL STREET WAY

This type of stock selection requires analysis using different ratios with a much deeper understanding of companies financials to know where to look. Using this method screens all stocks and allows an investor to scale it down to select ideas using variables like market capitalization, price, and growth, among others. The best way to look for companies that accomplish this is to establish criteria, followed by using a stock screener. A stock screener is an online tool used to automatically match up the exact criteria to find the ideal stocks, which will result in many to choose from. It has tools such as finding a growth rate of 20% or more the last five years or pays a high dividend over 3.5%. It could also include high/low P/E dependent if the investor is seeking growth or value. You may be thinking right now you don't know what to look for, and that's ok. I will address those concerns.

Side Story #2 – After earning my undergraduate degree in 2005 from the University of Central Florida (UCF) and getting my first real job out of college, I noticed every time I went to this new restaurant for lunch, it was packed wall-to-wall. It was pretty new in the area, but was always busy regardless of the day or time. I should have jumped in then on the company, but didn't connect the dots. Remember my point earlier about observation and how important it can be? This and the previous story relate exactly to this key point. It was a place that made a very efficient process that was able to get customers in and out by using an assembly line. That place was Chipotle Mexican Grill (CMG), and its stock traded in the $50-$60 range in 2006 when the IPO first came out. Check out its stock price today, and you will see what I mean by missing out on the opportunity. This will happen numerous times in your life, and by just by paying attention, you'll know a great idea when you *see it (as will the rest of the consumer base). As of June 2020, the stock was trading over $800 per share.*

HEADS UP BOOK CHANGES AHEAD

STOCK SCREENERS

The two stock screeners that I would recommend are products by Yahoo and Finviz. The screener tool is built using several metrics, ratios, and requirements. Basically, the stock screener is an online tool that investors can use to sift through specific ratios and select different stocks based on the criteria. For example, investors can look at investment options like market capitalization, P/E ratio, EPS, dividend yield, and the high and low trading price of the year (52 week highs and lows). Here's a simple example using the following ratios in Finviz such as Market Cap: Large, Dividend Yield: Over 3%, P/E: Over 15, EPS Growth next 5 years: Positive, and Sales Growth: Positive. Once the list is generated, scan through the list to see recognizable companies to research further.

It can also offer up analyst projections (see below) based on growth rates and EPS growth rates. Yahoo and Finviz offer easy to use stock screeners (and both are FREE) that can be used to find stocks that fit personal investment style. There are many other options available to simply Google "stock screener", but these two are the ones that I use the most today because of their easy usability. These aforementioned tips will certainly help. Below is an example of using the stock screener above and selecting MMM, and scrolling down to see the analyst projections.

Index	DJIA S&P500	P/E	17.41	EPS (ttm)	8.52	Insider Own	0.10%	Shs Outstand	588.05M	Perf Week	-3.42%
Market Cap	87.27B	Forward P/E	16.63	EPS next Y	8.03	Insider Trans	-6.10%	Shs Float	574.51M	Perf Month	7.61%
Income	4.97B	PEG	12.36	EPS next Q	1.78	Inst Own	70.00%	Short Float	1.30%	Perf Quarter	-5.23%
Sales	32.35B	P/S	2.70	EPS this Y	-14.80%	Inst Trans	-0.13%	Short Ratio	1.51	Perf Half Y	-10.06%
Book/sh	17.59	P/B	8.44	EPS next Y	10.31%	ROA	11.50%	Target Price	150.47	Perf Year	-19.88%
Cash/sh	7.61	P/C	19.49	EPS next 5Y	1.41%	ROE	48.50%	52W Range	114.04 - 187.72	Perf YTD	-15.88%
Dividend	5.88	P/FCF	38.58	EPS past 5Y	0.90%	ROI	16.30%	52W High	-20.85%	Beta	1.00
Dividend %	3.96%	Quick Ratio	1.20	Sales past 5Y	0.20%	Gross Margin	47.60%	52W Low	30.13%	ATR	4.96
Employees	96163	Current Ratio	1.70	Sales Q/Q	2.70%	Oper. Margin	20.50%	RSI (14)	50.94	Volatility	3.74% 2.74%
Optionable	Yes	Debt/Eq	2.22	EPS Q/Q	46.80%	Profit Margin	15.40%	Rel Volume	0.45	Prev Close	148.60
Shortable	Yes	LT Debt/Eq	1.90	Earnings	Apr 28 BMO	Payout	67.20%	Avg Volume	4.91M	Price	148.40
Recom	3.20	SMA20	1.05%	SMA50	3.33%	SMA200	-8.18%	Volume	2,229,849	Change	-0.13%

Stock screeners help take a large field of stocks and narrow it down to companies that meet exact objectives and criteria. The screener will help indicate how the company has been performing depending on the specific time period being researched. In about 5-10 pages I provide an idea of how to use these screeners effectively with some examples in the investment strategy. There are far too many things to cover, so I've just chosen a few below to help with some brief over-viewing and learning.

There are other factors that will affect how a stock is performing that doesn't show up on a stock screener, and investors should be aware of these factors. What else can affect a company's performance? A company's performance can highly fluctuate depending on several factors. One of those factors includes each earnings release (which most companies report quarterly every year on how they are doing). During this release, company's will highlight their future expectations of growth, which is forward looking, and can drastically impact the stock price. Other factors include a company news release, analysts revising their expectations, insider trading, and economic conditions. Before I move forward, let's revisit another example and then revisit some of those factors in further detail.

Side Story #3 – When I was completing my MBA in 2012, one of our final projects was to complete a full company analysis. I had always steered my teams throughout the program to research companies that I was either already invested in or that were on my radar of potential investments. So, I chose Coca-Cola (KO) as my company to research, as I had already been investing with them for over two years. When running all the full company analyses, the most common comparison naturally came up against PepsiCo (PEP), as the two companies have the soda market cornered as an oligopoly. After running the financial ratios (P/E, EPS, Profit Margin, etc.) I saw that Coca-Cola, in 2012, was a more profitable company. That validated my investment and even got me an A on the paper. One point still held firm that could not be found in my research paper. I have always known that people close to me are addicted to Diet Coke. I mean literally addicted like cigarettes to the point where they must have one a day to function. That piece of evidence was as good as any for me to steer my investment towards a solid company that would provide consistent future earnings.

HEADS UP BOOK CHANGES AHEAD

BREAKING DOWN THE EFT WAY

There's a new technique to investing I discovered recently that has been proved very successful called Breaking down the EFT. What does this mean in plain English? As a savvy investor, it gets easier to spot a growing trend or sector that should perform well over the next 12-24 months, or better yet, a future trend to invest in. This means finding companies poised to break out that are producing a growing product or technology. Some examples include Artificial Intelligence, Cyber Security, Robotics, and Life Science. Let me preface, this is an advanced technique because of the analysis that must be performed after identifying, analyzing, and synthesizing through the data.

Breaking down the ETF is a process of recognizing an industry (technology, manufacturing), a trend (artificial intelligence, data analysis), or market segment (small cap growth), reviewing the companies that make up that ETF, and analyzing stocks to find opportunities to invest. That sounds like a lot in one sentence. It is a lot of work. Don't worry. I'll break it down step by step and show an output of what to expect at the end and better yet, what type of results that can be found by using this technique. The example I'll use will break down an existing ETF in today's market, with finding an opportunity that yielded over 50% return in one stock in six months, followed by a 12% return and 20% return on two other stocks across on ETF. Let's go through the specifics how to on using this type of strategy.

In general, I review my portfolio at least annually for performance, opportunities, and just trying to answer an overall question, is it performing / constructed the way I intended. In 2017, I began re-analyzing my portfolio. Despite the fact that my portfolio was up over 20% later in the year, I felt I left opportunity on the table given the stock market's performance. One name in particular that I thought should be performing much better was an

ETF I liked called HACK. HACK is an ETF made up of cyber security stocks where the main objective is to prevent cybersecurity hacks. I owned the ETF for 2+ years and had made only modest gains (about 10% annually over three years totaling ~30%) in a sector I considered to be growing given the information in the news surround cyber security threats.

Many major companies suffered severe hacks or threats over the past 5 years, and I thought I had a winner on this trend. The problem with my investment was it had too many wildcards, risks, and underperforming companies in the ETF that weren't rotated out frequently enough. I originally wrote about HACK in my website blog in May 2017 and again talked about it on my podcast in September 2017. I first recommended HACK as it trading around 25-29 at the time and after a few years it hadn't made much movement and was underperforming with the risk I was taking. I thought my idea was right on point, but taking a little too long to mature. Most consumers can point to at least one data breach they read about (Equifax breach in 2017 had over 143 million consumers identities being stolen). Did you know in December 2017 alone there were over 20 data breaches that didn't reach the global news with brands like Nissan, Paypal, and Uber that were impacted. That all happened in just one month. The rest of the year wasn't much better standing at over 1,100 data breaches across all companies, with more than 171 million records exposed. These are the types of trends I started thinking through with research three years earlier. It's funny in one hand, my forward thinking was right, but on the other, I could've done a lot better. So that's the background on the ETF called HACK where my research led me to believe I should change my thinking on the subject.

So again, what's most interesting is the direction of the research was right, but needed a serious tweak to take advantage of an obvious growing market. Instead of looking at other EFT investments, I decided to dig a little deeper. I thought that if I looked under the hood even further at the ETF holdings to identify what made it up, identify what companies were performing well, and weed out which were struggling, I could find better opportunity.

Step 1 - identify the sector, industry, or trend to research further on competing companies as a potential investment. Remember, talked about this with Fidelity's stock screener and using their Themes feature. Here's the website just in case, click on Start a screen and locate Themes. In my example, Cyber Security is the trend I was following. The goal is to think through the industries, subjects, interests, or whatever you think is the next big thing and go study it. Future looking theories don't only live in the minds of others or talking heads on TV. Consumers that are educated with knowing what works/doesn't work can lead to the right discovery. Always remember, you're a much more sophisticated consumer that you think.

Step 2 - locate a Theme or ETF that has a collection of these investments. For example, I googled Cyber Security ETFs, and started to comb through them. Go ahead, type in Cyber Security ETF in Google and see what comes up. Upon searching, I found two prominent ETF names, HACK and CIBR, followed by a troll of others. HACK contains 50 holdings while CIBR has 32 holdings as of June 2018. Both ETFs demonstrated similar returns over the past three years, +30% ROI, and contained some of the same holdings. Thinking back, I believe I first read about HACK in doing research in Fortune magazine. Afterwards, I started to research the topic of cyber security and how CEOs were thinking it was their biggest challenges in the coming 3-5 years with investments. That sparked my interest.

Step 3 – after finding the ETF on ETF.com, I then went to download the holdings. Use the download feature to grab as much data as possible about the companies contained in the ETF based on the theme in Fidelity or industry. Once the holdings section is located, click view all holdings, copy all the holdings, and paste it into Excel. See screenshots below for the example.

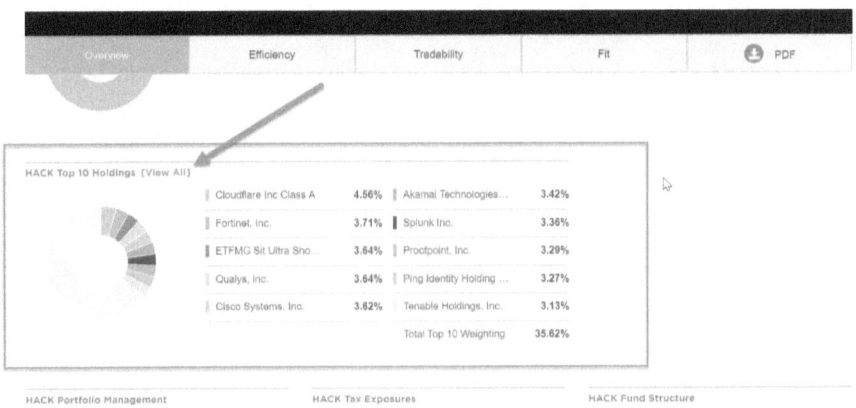

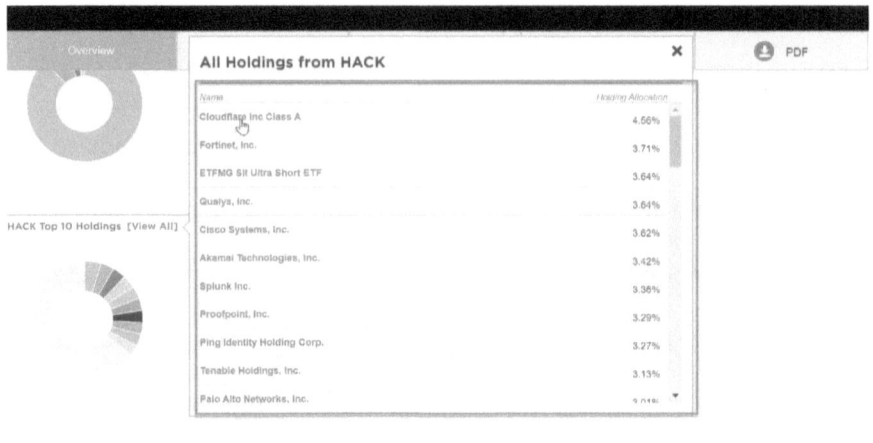

Step 4 - fill in the blanks with additional information needs that match up to my investment indicators that can be found later in the book in Chapter 12. All the information can be found in both finance.yahoo.com and Finviz.com. Trust me, it's a lot of work and information, but its ready to analyze, it makes a much more educated investor to understand how to read the differences. The ratios and variables to gather include:

- Market Capitalization - this helps understand the size of the company in relation to others in the stock market as it relates to risk.

- YTD return / 1 yr return - identify how the company has performed against internal / macro expectations.

- P/E Ratio - price to earnings ratio, this will help determine how the company fared vs. the overall market - check the market P/E ratio, use a simple Google search - S/P P/E ratio with S&P 500 or Dow Jones, both were around 25 in 2017. If the company being researched is over 25, it should grow faster than the market, if under 25, then it signals slower growth.

- Forward P/E Ratio - compared against current P/E ratio to identify if the company is expecting higher/lower growth in the next 12 months than previous 12 months.

- PEG Ratio - Price to earnings to growth ratio, considered a more complete picture than just P/E. Below one is desired, but must be compared against P/E to review for growth.

- Current ratio - is the balance sheet healthy. If the company is under 1.0 (generally not good), I expect big growth and the revenue model must be justified.

- ROE - How much profit was generated with shareholder money. Useful for comparing profitability of one company to another, however; if ROE is low, the company could be in the midst of a growth or breakout cycle.

- Profit margin - how much is the company earning, obviously higher the better.

- EPS Growth next year - If the company is planning on growing, this should be positive.

- EPS Growth next 5 years - same thing, just stretched over 5 years.

- Company update - look at news outlets to find out what's going on lately. Chipotle went through a long stretch of declining sales because of an E-Coli breakout. DuPont & Chemours had a $300+ million lawsuit because of contaminated water. Facebook was in the news for privacy concerns. These things happen, but keep in mind the events in general, are temporary.

The last piece cannot be understated as it follows one of my basic principles. That basic principle is to understand the company and how it makes money. Why is this so important? It's important significant news surfaces to understand how negative or positive news can impact company profits, the industry, and the business model. News and company updates can drive the company forward or pull it down. It can showcase how the business will evolve. It plays into why the company is impacted by macro trends, industry trends, or other things that impact the company.

After all this data is collected, now what? Start analyzing it, identify what stands out, where are the biggest differences in the data. In my example of breaking down the Cybersecurity ETF, HACK, I easily identified several companies. Take a look at the screenshot of spreadsheet provided. The items that I see of identifiable areas to see is the difference / balance between current and future P/E ratio. Take a look at MANT. The stock had a very close assimilation of current P/E vs. future P/E. The PEG ratio was by second highest of its peers at 10.21. It also showcased a decent return ~9% with a decent chance of breaking out if they could beat earnings. It's a good bet if they beat earnings to invest in given the rest of the financials except for ROE. CUDA was another solid bet that worked out well. I invested into the stock, only to have it bought out by a larger competitor, netting a 40%+ return on investment as the competitor paid a higher premium. Remember, all the financials need to be taken into consideration. A negative ROE could indicate the company has invested significantly into research and won't generate significant gains for years. In the screenshot below, take FTNT for example, it had a -223% ROE, return on equity, had a ~30% return despite the negative ROE. As I stated, all of the ratios need to be taken into consideration when evaluating the investments.

Symbol	Top 25 Holdings	% Portfoli	Shares	Shares	Country	MkCap	YTD Retur	Any latest	P/E	Forward P	PEG	Current R	ROE	Profit Mar	EPS Grow	EPS Grow	Oc
AKAM	Akamai Technologies Inc	4.75	1043997	-5756	United Sta	8.7	-24.07	Trending	28.93	18.58	2.27	3.1	9.5	12.7	2.71	12.65	
FEYE	FireEye Inc	4.72	2999587	-16548	United Sta	3.19	51.09	Up large t				2.1	-41	-46.4	90.5	15	
JNPR	Juniper Networks Inc	4.66	1804038	-9952	United Sta	10.4	1.66		17.02	11.62	1.2	2.5	13.1	12.5	5.14	13.57	
CSCO	Cisco Systems Inc	4.59	1525522	-8416	United Sta	166	15.42		17.76	13.35	1.72	3	14.9	20	-9.8	10.24	
TMICY	Trend Micro Inc	4.55	1014701	-5600	Japan	7.2	36.7		31.4					18.69			
SYMC	Symantec Corp	4.54	1518285	-8376	United Sta	19.4	42.93			15.52		1	-10.2	-8.7	12.67	1.9	
SOPH	Sophos Group PLC	4.54	6752756	-37256	United Kin	2.7	119.79										
CUDA	Barracuda Networks Inc	4.49	1981835	-10932	United Sta	1.4	20.91		136.37	29.65	12.01	1		2.8	14.81	11.4 bo	
QLYS	Qualys Inc	4.42	920038	-5124	United Sta	1.9	70.3		52.84	49.52	2.94	2.5	14.7	18.9	20.8	17	
GIMO	Gigamon Inc	4.38	1127593	-6220	United Sta	1.5	-10.98		587.88	34.07	19.6	3.7	1.1	1	42.55	30 bo	
CYBR	CyberArk Software Ltd	4.36	1152129	-6356	Israel	1.5	-6.26		54.68	32.46	3.53	3.7	9.1	11.9	24.59	15.3	
PANW	Palo Alto Networks Inc	4.32	333431	-1836	United Sta	13.8	17.85			36.6		1.6	-26.5	-12.3	23.7	23.53	
SPLK	Splunk Inc	4.24	714856	-3940	United Sta	8.9	30.69			78.2		2	-44.6	-32.7	51.67	44.73	
FTNT	Fortinet Inc	4.24	1278584	-7052	United Sta	6.7	29.58		106.69	33.7	5.32	1.8	7.5	4.7	19.6	19.76	
PFPT	Proofpoint Inc	4.24	518523	-2860	United Sta	4.1	33.33			92.12		1.5	-223.9	-21	55.25	25	
IMPV	Imperva Inc	4.15	1053467	-5812	United Sta	1.4	18.23			45.89		2.5	-0.8	-0.7	-32.9	16.27	
BAESY	BAE Systems PLC	1.41	1907972	-10524	United Kin	26.4	5.78		18.41								
BAH	Booz Allen Hamilton Holding Cc	1.07	312828	-1724	United Sta	5.6	5.91		21.54	18.57	2.48	1.6			6.27	8.73	
MIME	Mimecast Ltd	1.06	395852	-2184	United Sta	1.6	66.59			149.74		1.4	-9.3	-3.7	232	25	
MANT	Mantech International Corp Cla	1.03	252308	-1392	United Sta	1.8	8.97		30.07	28.85	10.21	2.3	4.7	3.6	5.74	2.09	

Please keep in mind this is an advanced technique and I wouldn't recommend it for a passive investor. It's an advanced strategy for someone that is looking to create an edge and is willing to put in the extra work. It's for an investor looking to eek out more gains that will benefit their investment strategy. It takes time, research, and discipline with an analytical mindset. I don't think I can stress enough that this is an advanced technique for those that want to spend the time that's needed to invest in using a strategy like this instead of being just a passive investor. Before moving on, here's one more example going through the ETF, ROBO, which is made up of companies targeting robotics, automation, and Big Data.

What's so important about ROBO, the ETF? As I'm writing this in 2020, given how far we've come as a society with many "smart devices", the natural progression is very much about what to do with all that data. Big Data, to be more accurate. Over the next 10-20 years, many experts and trends are all pointing the same direction, more connectivity, more Bluetooth capabilities, 5G connections, and smart connected homes. The smart connected homes and cities are a game changer for consumers and investors, check this article for more info. In the next 10 years, experts are predicting the majority of households will have smart everything such as thermostats, televisions people can talk and interact, smart lighting, smart refrigerators. What about other devices? Smart appliances to ensure cooking is done at the right time/temperature, smart mattresses to regulate sleeping at the right firmness, smart wardrobes to help keep up with trends and feeling good, smart showers to regulate to the most preferred temperature, and much more. Oh yeah, not to mention all of these devices can be controlled with voice controls and all that data will be incredibly valuable to marketers in the future.

Getting back to ROBO, well everything described would need ROBO companies to connect it all with doing some investment analysis. Analysis will come in the form of Big Data, Analytics, and companies that will literally do nothing else but try and figure out how to use all the data to better target consumers for future sales. Some of the top companies in ROBO, who are they?

- Nvidia (NVDA) - Nvidia provides advanced semiconductors for gaming, special effects, and artificial intelligence for platforms designed to connect data in a thoughtful approach.
- iRobot (IRBT) - iRobot designs, builds, and sells robots for consumers designed to make people's life better with more advanced solutions (vacuuming, lawn care, learning) on automated systems.
- Rockwell Automation (ROK) - ROK - Rockwell automation provides industrial automation and digital

transformation solutions including analytical software for companies to make smarter decisions.

- Intuitive Surgical (ISRG) - Intuitive Surgical designs and manufactures robotic surgical instruments & systems that enable surgeons to perform various surgeries. Their technology makes surgeries safer, speeds up recovery, and reduce costs to hospitals and again, is based on robotics and data intelligence.

- Splunk (SPLK) - Splunk provides software for companies to gain operational intelligence to act on data quickly with strong data management capabilities.

Here's my spreadsheet breaking them down with more analysis:

Name	Ticker	Shares	Market	% of M.	% of Ne	What they	MkCap	Price	YTD Re	Any latest	P/E	Forwar	PEG	Current	ROE
NVIDIA CORP	NVDA	94239	23183736	1%	1%	GPU & Tegra	140	240	62%		68	33.23	5.45	8.4	24%
QUALCOMM INC	QCOM	366427	20776411	1%	1%	Semiconduct	103	88.7	54%		24.76	14.52	0.92	1.0	98%
INTUITIVE SURGICAL INC	ISRG	101634	46857330	2%	2%	davinci produ	69	589	22%		55.07	42.25	4.59	4.6	18%
DEERE & CO	DE	137677	20286706	1%	1%	John Deere e	55	175.9	8%		17.7	15.87	1.29		28%
ILLUMINA INC	ILMN	37151	12190729	0.951	0.953	genetics anal	48	329.42							
AUTODESK INC	ADSK	165904	22551331	1%	1%	AudoCad, de	40.5	182	42%		309.11	41.4		0.6	-71.70%
MICROCHIP TECHNOLOGY INC	MCHP	233624	21846180	1%	1%	Manufacture	26.7	109.29	42%		80.3	17.51	22.36	0.9	7%
XILINX INC	XLNX	303226	21526014	1%	1%	Programmabl	25.5	99.18	10%		27.31	27.4	3.62	6.4	35%
ROCKWELL AUTOMATION INC	ROK	240714	43338140	2%	2%	architecture,	22	205.64	35%		25.51	20.28	2.09	2.1	18%
ServiceNow	NOW					Cloud service	21.4	281	50%		1700	71.21	56.61	1	3%
VOCERA COMMUNICATIONS INC	VCRA	756966	15631348	1%	1%	communicatic	20.89	20.89	-50%		45.87			4.3	-11%
CADENCE DESIGN SYS INC	CDNS	582025	23880488	1%	1%	Automation s	20.6	72.28	64%		47.77	30.94	4.34	1.7	31%
IPG PHOTONICS CORP	IPGP	182958	46191406	2%	2%	laser product	13	144	13%		31.71	25.87	2.64	9.5	19%
TELEDYNE TECHNOLOGIES INC	TDY	119030	23316787	1%	1%	digital imagin	13	361	65%		35.8	32.34	1.23	1.5	16%
NORDSON CORP	NDSN	165179	22163718	1%	1%	Automated di	9.4	162	33%		27.6	23.16	2.12	1.5	23%
PTC INC	PTC	286431	24174778	1%	1%	IoT, Solutions	8.8	75.84	-9%			25.96	9.05	1.2	-2%
ZEBRA TECHNOLOGIES CORP-C	ZBRA	322172	50271719	2%	2%	automatic ide	8	255	47%		43.32	14.75	4.33	1.1	14%
QIAGEN N.V.	QGEN	668157	23182804	1%	1%	Transform bi	7.8	33.68	-10%			32.7		2.4	-1%
COGNEX CORP	CGNX	795543	38400861	2%	2%	Automation c	7.8	54	43%		54.5	54.13	3.63	7.7	14%

Some of the companies I came across based on the fundamental analysis (financial ratios) and comparison against their peers are: Autodesk (ADSK), Rockwell Automation (ROK), Zebra Technologies (ZBRA), and Cognex (CGNX). I outlined these companies for specific reasons, such as:

- All had a market capitalization under 50 billion, signaling smaller companies that have more room to grow. Example, it's easier to double growth from 5 to 10 billion, vs. 100 to 200 billion within a growth model.

- The types of industries the companies operate in and what they do. The companies collectively have features I really like cloud based services (lower hard costs) and automation services.

- All had positive returns the previous year, all in double digits.

- They are expecting EPS growth next year and over the next 5 years (more growth, more expansion) with strong PEG ratios.

- All have positive profit margins.

- I researched all the companies and dug enough into their business models, management teams, and got more intelligence into how they tick, work, and make money.

This part may seem easier once the research is done, but it's only because the all the data collection and analysis has been compiled to look meaningful. Robotics, automation, business intelligence/analytics, and Big Data are all important themes. If you agree, then I strongly encourage to review ROBO and do more research. All the research I've read seems to point towards seems to point towards the biggest revolution of intelligence since the last wave of Google with SEO and Facebook with targeted advertising. Smarter everything is coming and the ability to take advantage of it with the right investment ideas is the key. The next few areas touch upon variables to be aware of with investing that can impact the stock performance.

EARNINGS ANNOUNCEMENT

Publicly traded companies on Wall Street report earnings on a quarterly basis. The key part to this statement is that they all report at different times of the month depending on the financial cycle implemented when their company was formed. Each time a company reports earnings, they either miss, meet, or beat the street projections (Wall Street analyst consensus). *This is the top indicator of why a company's stock moves up or down*. Now, if a company meets or misses EPS (earnings per share) expectations by $.01, it begs the question, what the big deal is. Why is one penny such a big deal? Spread that penny over the millions or billions of shares the company has outstanding (publicly owned), and it shows how that can be a big deal.

Something else could have happened as well. The company could beat the earnings estimates, but issue guidance of lower future projected earnings, which could negatively impact the stock. For example, if Chipotle (CMG) beats earnings, but their same store future estimates are down, then it could affect future earnings growth and the stock price negatively. This is known as a leading indicator for future growth. This is directly correlated to an early forewarning of lower future growth rates, which equals a slowdown of the company. If a company has a strong history of meeting or beating expectations, then likely the stock price will get a nice increase in market value along with the investors of the stock.

COMPANY RELEASE

Sometimes if companies know in advance that something will drastically impact earnings (positively or negatively), they release the information in advance to warn Wall Street and investors. The strategic advantage for this is to allow analysts to adjust expectations to accurately prepare the investment community. A few examples of this type of activity would be if the company lost or gained a major customer, had slowed revenues, or was impacted by forces beyond its control (recession, bad crops, or even a natural disaster in worst cases). The most recent example of this came in 2020 with COVID-19. Several companies went on the offensive to prepare Wall Street before their earnings by issuing negative guidance. This means they wanted to be proactive with negative news.

In general, company releases in advance of earnings are viewed as negative on future earnings. However, from time to time, a company will release something about a breakthrough technology that will propel the company to new heights. An example would be if a pharmaceutical company announces it has found the cure for disease "x" or its new drug has been green-lighted by the FDA. This would naturally propel the stock to higher estimates because it would be a signal of significant future growth caused by a new income stream. As an expected result, the company stock price would naturally rise from such an event or announcement.

ANALYST REVISING ESTIMATES

This is similar to a company release as it is generally found in the public sector on news and notes of a company. The biggest difference is that analysts are outside the company and make their revisions based on new information acquired that requires them to change the estimate. Another reason to make an adjustment to earnings is a press release (similar to company release statements). As a rule of thumb, an upward adjustment signals positive news for a company, whereas a downward modification signals a negative sign.

INSIDER TRADING

Before I jump into this topic, I'd like to preface that not all insider trading is illegal, regardless of what's been heard on TV. Companies compensate executives with stock options that they can be exercised after a number of years, or if the stock reaches a specific target. Insider trading can be tracked just like any other public record when company officials make purchases or sales. Generally, if the top executives in a firm are buying their company stock, they believe the future growth is going higher than what the market currently shows. This is a good buying signal for investors. Here's a website that investors can utilize to periodically check-in for their investments – InsiderTracking.com.

Top company executives have the inside track on everything going on within the company, so they should know a thing or two about it. Similar to buying, selling company stock can also signal a potential downshift in the company's immediate future; however, don't be fooled. This may or may not be true, as just like the rest of us, executives have life obligations such as sending their kids to college or closing on a house purchase and may need the money for something similar. Most companies today have strict rules in place when executives can and cannot trade their stock to prevent collusion from internal information to protect the public and the firm. These types of rules are governed by the Securities and Exchange Commission (SEC) to provide a greater level of protection for the company, its employees, its shareholders, and the individuals making the purchase or sale.

ECONOMIC CONDITIONS / NEWS RELEASES

The last item here, economic conditions, may have a positive or adverse effect on an investment, depending on the state of the economy. There are so many macro factors that individual companies have no control over that could swing a stock and the market as much as 3-10% in a single day. Remember earlier, I had mentioned a few major economic events in the past 25 years – The Internet Bubble Burst in the late 90s, the Housing Crash in 2007, and COVID-19? These events decreased the overall valuation of the entire stock market with major declines. This occurred regardless of how well companies were performing during that time period. Events like these are anomalies nor should they long term investment strategy.

Lastly, news releases can also impact short term stock performance. The challenge with news releases is even if they don't mention specific stocks at all, but do reference an industry as a whole or a direct competitor, it could an indirect impact. Here's a good example. In 2013, natural gas prices had unexpected benefits due to the companies involved in successfully discovering more natural gas in the United States with fracking for oil. This had an extremely positive effect on just about anything that dealt with natural gas, from the discovery to producing vehicles that run on natural gas. All stocks related to natural gas in some form moved up around 15-20% overall (some much higher) during that time period.

During periods of uncertainty in the national or global markets, there are still strategies that can be utilized for investing. Remember the example provided earlier regarding Joe the Farmer? Joe routinely bought cows at different prices over time regardless of the economic environment. Keep that same strategy in mind for this situation as dollar cost averaging still works. Another very helpful stock strategy for uncertainty is using sell stops to reduce potential downside in stocks. I discuss this in further detail in the next chapter.

Chapter Ten

_____

GROWTH INVESTING VS.
VALUE INVESTING

T he next few sections of the book are broken down to help explain the market overall and what the different verbiage means. This will help with understanding more about companies and more importantly for research, including stock screeners. I think to get us to a better understanding, we should start with questions to help gain some perspective on market specific verbiage:

- Do you know Market Capitalization (Market Cap)?

- How about how companies are split into different market caps?

- What about Growth vs. Value investing?

- What about the difference between Growth vs. Value investing?

- What about how a portfolio is diversified, what does that mean?

This is all common language I want investors to understand to accurately use the growing investment knowledge. Anyone with a 401k plan or have even heard from friends, co-workers, or parents talk about it, odds are you've been exposed to some of these terms above. If the 401k is a foreign concept, trust me, that time will come. This section will help determine how to pick between the many options offered by the employer's provider.

These are important concepts to understand. Learning it now will prove more beneficial instead of checking with the closest cube-mate to make investment decisions. All this decisions will influence future retirement plans. Let's dive into classifying a stock with its market capitalization to bring clarity to these concepts and create a general understanding of them. As a disclosure, a common technique I won't be covering in the book to keep our concepts simple revolve around Technical Investing. To learn more about different investment styles, check out the other books I recommend in Chapter 13.

MARKET CAPITALIZATION (MARKET CAP)

Market capitalization characterizes the total valuation of a company. Why does it matter? Market caps matter because they provide insight into a balanced portfolio, based on the size of the company, for diversification. Market caps are spread into buckets, ranging from Mega Cap worth over $200 billion (like Apple or Google) to Micro Caps worth under $150 million (like INVE, a security and data company). The bigger the market cap, the more stable the company is, in general. Likewise, the smaller the company, the bigger the risk and possible upside as well. The entire purpose for talking about market caps is for diversification as it relates to a balanced portfolio and spreading out risks and taking risks as well.

The technical definition of market caps is the term represents the total number of outstanding shares multiplied by the current stock price. For more info on this, I suggest researching the current information on the stock, which can always be found on their 10-K, or here at SEC Edgar (Securities and Exchange Commission). For a faster approach, let's attack it just like most things in life by using the internet to make this process easier to follow.

The internet has made searching for the appropriate information much easier today than it was years ago. For example, rather than looking it up and searching with SEC Edgar, it's just as easy to lookup the company on Yahoo Finance (www.yahoo.com/finance). Type in the symbol, and look under the Summary section of the stock for the market capitalization using the bullets below.

- $200 billion or more = Mega Cap
- $10 billion – $200 billion = Large Caps
- $1.5 billion - $10 billion = Mid Caps
- $150 million - $1.5 billion = Small Caps
- Under $150 million = Micro Caps

Since stock prices fluctuate daily, as a result, market cap also fluctuate. This doesn't mean companies change market caps frequently, but can cause a change in valuation over time. For example, Coca-Cola (KO) has 4.3 billion shares outstanding, and their stock price in June 2020 was around 45 dollars per share, giving them a market cap of 193 billion. This would make KO just shy of being a mega cap stock, but still falls into the large cap group.

Next, I review the common characteristics of each market cap to help further illustrate the differences between each one.

LARGE & MEGA CAP STOCKS

Large and mega cap stocks tend to be more stable than that of a smaller or mid-cap. One of several factors is consistent sales in a high volume capacity, given the size, and the company has sustained market fluctuations, recessions, and economic conditions to remain consistently efficient. During that period, they have grown significantly to reach between $10-$200+ billion in market capitalization. Their revenue and growth rates offer stability vs. some of the other market caps, which tends to classify them as blue chips. These market caps represent the lowest amount of risk compared with the lower market caps.

There are exceptions to these characteristics such as Facebook (FB) that is only 10 years old as a company and is already a mega cap (Reminder: Facebook went public in 2013, but has been growing and established as a company long before they became a publicly traded company). Consider others like Proctor & Gamble (PG), AT&T (T), and Exxon Mobile (XOM). These companies make up the typical description of a long standing company that sustained through decades. They were able to accomplish it with a combination of consistent management teams and stability. Their management teams know how to consistently remain profitable and sustainable as a company. Another common characteristic among a majority of the companies within group, is most tend to pay a dividend. This creates yet another way to measure their growth and future value of the stock.

Since most large and mega caps pay dividends, this is an excellent opportunity to introduce how to calculate an expected return with a dividend that remains consistent. This provides a formula on how to project and calculate returns on stocks. The dividend method is one of several ways. This is done as an offshoot of using the Gordon's Dividend Growth Model as a consistent method to evaluate stocks. The Dividend Growth Model calculates a fair price for a stock in the marketplace and looks something like this $P = D1/r-g$. It basically takes the future dividend (D1) and divides it over the difference between the expected growth rate (g) and the dividend growth rate (r).

This is not something I expect beginners to calculate right away to determine fair market value for a stock. It's important because it leads to calculating the expected shareholder's rate of return. The return is something to care about because it relates to the potential return that can be expected.

DIVIDEND GROWTH RATE FORMULA

The expected shareholder rate of return is an easy formula that looks like this:

$$k = \frac{D0(1+g)}{P0} + g$$

- D0 is the annual dividend paid last year (easy to find in Statistics section of Yahoo Finance)
- g is the discount growth rate, or the rate expected to return at least – most large cap companies use between 7-10%
- P0 is the current stock price (Summary section of Yahoo Finance)
- k is the expected shareholder rate of return

Dealing with predictable companies like Wal-Mart (WMT) that routinely pay and raise their dividends is great for predicting the potential ROI. It's easy because their growth rates are derived from the latest dividend and what the stock should be trading at in one year. To put this exercise into action, let's take a look at an example.

Let's take an example such as PepsiCo (PEP) in 2013. At the end of June 2020, the stock price of PEP was $135 per share with a dividend of $0.955 per share ($0.955 x 4 quarters (one year) = $3.82 annual). The quarterly dividend last year was $0.9275 ($3.71 annually, again $.9275 x 4 = $3.71). Take this direct knowledge and apply it to the future dividend of this year to find the projected growth rate. Meaning the next dividend should be (($3.82-$3.71)/3.71 = 2.96%) $3.82 x 1.0296 = $3.93 for next year. They actually raised the dividend to $1.0225, $4.09 per share, meaning it came out slightly higher than the expected dividend. This is great for an investor as it means the company is growing faster than the expected ROI. Let's take the materials above and plug it into the formula for the expected rate of return using 10% as minimum required return.

$$k = \frac{D0(1+g)}{P0} + g$$

$$k = \frac{3.71(1.10)}{135} + .10 = 13.02\%$$

That wasn't too hard now was it? It's literally just plugging in the numbers with an estimate of the company internal growth rate. 13.02% for any stock is definitely a good return for the shareholder. When calculating this in the future, remember to add the growth rate after calculating the above formula. This is especially valuable to use when a company has been paying a consistent dividend rate with steady increases over a long period of time. Large and mega cap companies fit this expectation as consistent models of success in the maturity stage of the product life cycle we discussed earlier.

To measure the rate of return of the portfolio vs. the market, there are specific benchmarks to review. Specific indexes are available that provide an accurate measure of the large cap stocks that have been established for a long time. These benchmarks serve as gauges on how the stock market is performing generally. The most identifiable measure / index of current large capitalization stocks is the Dow Jones Industrial Average (DJIA) that was created in 1896. This average is made up of 30 large cap stocks from various sectors that make up the average.

There is also another index called the Standard & Poor's 500 (SPX), which is a collection of 500 large cap stocks, created in 1957, that creates another average. Both are viewed as benchmarks for how the stock market is performing within a given time period. On financial TV channels that discusses the stock market, generally the DJIA or S&P 500 will be located on the bottom corners. The last one is the NASDAQ, which has 100 non-financial companies is more closely aligned to the technology sector. These symbols correlate to the daily measurement of the daily U.S. stock market performance.

MID-CAP STOCKS

This categorization of stocks was naturally created to create separation from outperforming small cap stocks and stocks that weren't quite as big as large cap. It really is a middle-ground group as they have better stability than small caps, but generally possess better growth potential than large caps. Some of the typical companies that are considered mid-cap companies are New York

Times (NYT), AutoNation (AN), Foot Locker (FL) and GrubHub (GRUB).

The S&P also has an index called the S&P Midcap 400 (IJJ) that has a broad reflection of mid cap stocks similar to the S&P 500 in large caps. Unlike the large cap performance measurements of the Dow Jones and S&P 500, the index for mid-caps and small caps won't be as widely promoted as the large cap sector. The rationale behind this is there are so many more mid and small cap companies vs. the large cap companies, and the indicator is less accurate for them and their performance.

SMALL CAP STOCKS

Small caps provide investors with a strong playing field of high growth stocks that are itching to get up to the levels of mid & large cap values. Rapid growth is possible when dealing with companies of this caliber because of their scale. It's much easier to grow faster and double revenues at $100 million, than if revenue is $100 billion. Small caps do carry a much greater risk than the larger cap companies as they provide better potential for high growth. Smaller companies operate this way because they don't have a full line of products developed yet. They tend to specialize in a smaller product line that is still evolving and aiming for many years of consistent sales.

There are two benchmarks that are utilized for an overall performance of the small cap sector. The first benchmark is the S&P 600 (SML), and the second is the Russell 2000 Index. Like the previous examples, S&P 600 contains 600 small cap companies of both growth and value (mostly growth) companies. The Russell 2000 Index is a well-balanced index of small cap stocks that provide a wide-ranging gauge for the small-cap segment. Like its counterparts, the Russell 2000 is modified each year to stay up to date. Small cap stocks are obvious targets for larger companies to acquire due to their ability to add new products to an existing product line. New products provide new growth potential with a pipeline of new products and ideas for larger companies to leverage which can keep them from getting stale. Small cap product lines can achieve huge earnings because their new products and services hit early product life cycle large caps generally lack.

MICRO CAP STOCKS

Any company that is generating under $150 million in revenue falls under this category of Micro Caps. This means there is very high risk, a potential for high reward, yet there's barely any coverage at the analyst level on Wall Street. This is because the amount of information is extremely limited with so many stocks to cover. The amount of shares outstanding is very low because these companies are in general new to the market with very limited professional analysis. Some people these to micro caps as the "Pink Sheets" stocks, stocks that trade for $5 or under. These types of stock require lots of patience and time to eventually bloom into even a small cap stock.

Since we now know how companies are segregated into market caps, or categories, let's continue to split them up further into growth vs. value investments or even mixed investments. This will really get us to a more educated level for fully understanding diversification. As we are getting further into investments with research, understanding more about investments, and classification, positions tend to appear in classification grids. They do this to visually see where it lives on the segregated market cap and style. The grids are very common and can be found in other publications that break down stocks/ETFs/Mutual Funds within the S&P, Bloomberg, and Kiplinger. See below for an example of the small cap value sector.

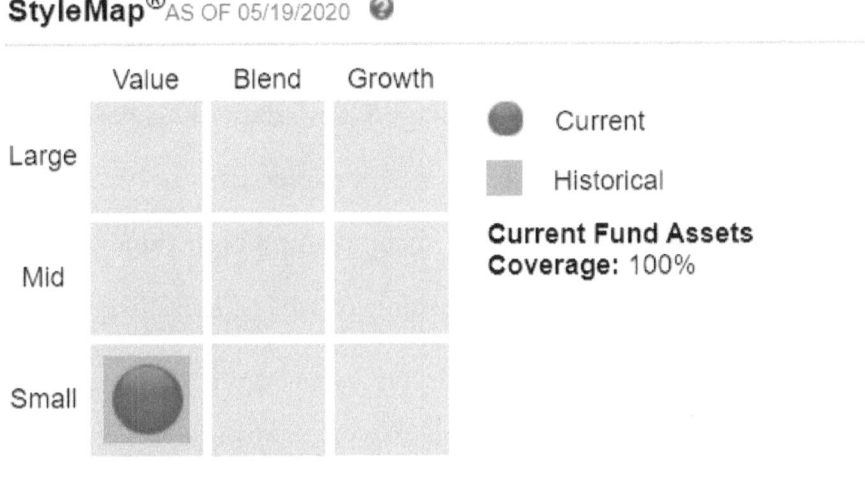

The grid serves to break up an investment idea, stock, or portfolio into market cap and growth or value investments. *This is very important to understand once we get into the portfolio and especially ETFs.* The grid will show where an individual investment or group of investments should be characterized. It's easier for investors to understand which market cap and segment they are investing in and this will allow them to make better decisions for their investment needs.

For example, if I've selected a <u>Large-Cap ETF, ITOT</u>, from the Fidelity platform, I should investigate things about the ETF to give me confidence for a possible investment. For example, let's say that ITOT, turns out to be a Large Cap Mixed. This means the investment contains a majority of companies that are valued over $10 billion and have segments encompassing both value and growth aspects. I provided a quick example of what it looks like the one above. above

My goal is that by using the grid above, it can visually help to see how a stock or portfolio is positioned from a risk, exposure, and growth/value perspective. We will now transition into how stocks can fit into either value, growth, or mixed segments to tie both of the above sections together. This will cover the second half of the criteria of evaluating a stock for growth or value.

VALUE INVESTING

Value investing is a good fit for investors who tend to be more risk adverse, who look for bargains, and who identify ways to stretch their dollar. Wait a second, I'm not talking about coupon cutting or shopping at a thrift store. People that have a natural tendency to look for sales, not pay full price, and go the extra mile for a deal naturally will love value stocks. Value investing is for those investors that look for undervalued situations just like stocks. An accepted method to define a value stock within a portfolio is if the current P/E (price to earnings) ratio is lower than its expected growth rate of its EPS (earnings per share). Another method that analysts use, is if the stock's P/E ratio is trading lower than the market average, it can be characterized as undervalued. Don't get scared with these terms; it's actually quite easy to find.

Remember earlier when we talked about using a stock screener? Here's where it comes into practical use. The risk is generally much lower for value stock investors than those looking at growth investing (again, this relates to looking for bargains and undervalued stocks). Also, these investments commonly pay dividends, are more mature in the product life cycle stage, and expectations are clear as to what type of ROI to expect from the investment.

Many investors think of value stocks in the same context as searching for bargains. The simple reason is in that when finding a bargain investment with upside that pays off, the reward is tremendous. An example of a value stock would be Caterpillar (CAT) in 2013 and again in 2015 because of several macroeconomic factors. Their short downswing the company encountered, along with several market reasons, led to a depressed stock price. To identify a value stock, here are some of the most common characteristics:

- The stock has hit a 52-week low (the lowest point the stock traded in the last year) or below its 200 day moving average (The average prices, high, low, and average during a 200 day period)
- Low P/E vs. industry norm, or competition
- PEG (Price to Earnings Growth) ratio is less than one, signaling the company is either slightly or very undervalued
- Last few earnings reports have dipped from expectations
- Higher projected earnings growth – next 1-5 years projections

None of those characteristics said the stocks were glaringly undervalued or cheap such as penny stocks (stocks trading under $5). According to the guidelines and criteria above, stocks that fit into this bucket are in fact undervalued according to the market or historical perspective. Value investors have potential lower outlooks for risk than growth stock investors. A very effective value investing strategy is to identify stocks that are undervalued and ride them until they become entirely valued correctly. Once properly valued, it could be a very healthy gain and ROI.

WHY DO STOCKS BECOME UNDERVALUED ANYWAY?

There are a number of reasons that we discussed earlier. The company could have missed sales projections, had an issue within their industry, or even experienced a temporary public relations problem causing the stock price to become depressed. Let's get back to an actual example of a value stock in July 2013. It's one we mentioned earlier, Caterpillar (CAT). Here's how we can tell right away that the stock is undervalued:

- 12 month trailing (current) P/E is 11.5 vs. the market or historical. Remember P/E equals (Current Stock Price/ EPS)

- EPS growth rate = 14.6%,

- By Definition = P/E < EPS Growth Rate, 11.5 < 14.6

- The 52 week low was 79.4, it was trading in 83-85 range, 52 week high is 99.7 (data was reported as of July 2013)

- Current P/E = 11.5, Industry Average = 10.8, S&P = 18.3

- PEG Ratio = .82

- Earnings – The company missed their earnings estimate three quarters in a row, Q4 2012, Q1 2013, Q2 2013

- The next six quarters the EPS projections were much higher than the current ratio – 33% projection higher than current EPS just in next two quarters

  - If looking at the averages overall, it's projected at 14.6% growth the rest of the year, and 15.9% growth next year

- Caterpillar also had problems internationally in China causing uncertainty in the company and instability in the stock price

There's something I want to point out in the exercise. Don't let all these numbers, ratios, and percentages be intimidating. I've discussed free stock screeners in the book and how to use them. Most of this information can be found at one of the stock screeners mentioned (Yahoo Stock Screener and Finviz.com). Using a stock screener to identify stocks that meet specific criteria to find opportunities on stocks that are undervalued is recommended. Let's take a look at the stock chart for Caterpillar (CAT) over the time periods 2012-2014 and 2016 for the value periods.

Caterpillar's 20-year Stock Chart

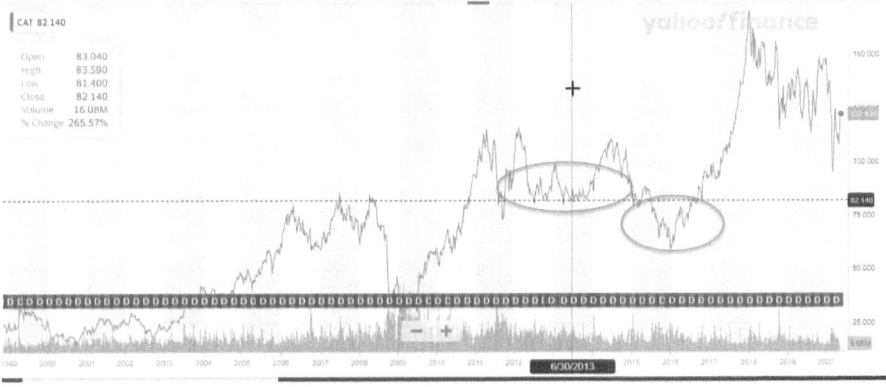

The stock chart above should be fairly easy to read. The horizontal access represents years and the vertical access represents stock price. Notice that in 2011 and mid-2012, the stock reached all-time highs around 120 per share which was either fairly-valued or over-valued (meaning it turned into a growth stock). The last highest touch point was in the beginning of 2012 around 115 per share, whereas it dipped into the 80s in mid-2013. The stock returned to normal form (fair value closer to 110), that resulted in a 20% gain, not to mention the dividend payout ratio that can picked up at a 2.8% current yield. That would be a total potential gain of 22.8% for an undervalued stock. Again, there was another opportunity in 2015-2016 in the second dip. Remember, buying undervalued stocks presents an opportunity to return to fair valuation.

One major thing to keep in mind when picking any investment, be sure to understand what the company does and how it makes money. Caterpillar (CAT) is a manufacturer of construction and mining equipment. Ever seen a CAT device? They are huge land movers. The company has a distribution advantage over their competition that falls along the lines with Coca-Cola's (KO) distribution network. Like Coca-Cola, Caterpillar has maintained a strategic advantage over their competition with their extensive distribution network. CAT guarantees 99% availability of their equipment worldwide delivered within 48 hours and most are delivered within 24 hours. Let's say a contractor is managing a multi-billion dollar construction job and need trustworthy equipment, reliability is paramount. Equipment delivery speed is a tremendous asset. Some construction managers that are in charge of multi-billion dollar projects and waiting an extra few days isn't an option. As I stated earlier, know the type of industry the company is in and what the company does to generate cash flow.

Just to emphasize enough understanding, let's review one more stock position that shows up as currently undervalued by using a stock screener (as of June 2020). I ran a stock screener using Yahoo! Finance Stock Screener with the following criteria and came up with a list of names. In the criteria drop-down menu, unless specified, the criteria will be ANY. Just keep in mind, unless searching for a specific industry, leave the criteria as ANY. Here's a run-through run to put this into practice:

- Share Price (Min) - $10 – Keep in mind I didn't want penny stocks (under $5). Penny stocks cause much higher risk and are not something we need to dip into.
- Market Cap (Min) - $2 billion to $10 billion – I wanted companies that are established
- Valuation
    - P/E Ratio – Over 5, this proves to be a pretty reliable range for undervalued stocks in general

- ○ PEG Ratio – Under 1, remember our rule from above, the PEG should be under 1.0 as it signifies undervalued
- Analysts Estimates – 5 years growth – Positive to signal positive outlet
- Select Find Stocks

This search provided many options to review and several companies that I was completely unfamiliar with their business model. Remember one of the rules above: know the company and know how it generates cash flow. There are two options here: either research a bunch of companies, or find ones that are known and understanding what they do. I opted for option two, and the first thing I did was look for companies I recognized so I could understand quickly how the company made money. Just on the first page, I noticed a few names I knew their business at a high level. The few companies I knew enough to investigate were Ally Financial (ALLY), H&R Block (HRB), Kemper Corporation (KMPR), and Tech Data Corporation (TECD). I decided to focus on ALLY, because I knew what that company did, the business model at a high level, and it fit my criteria. Let's go ahead and investigate further using the screener and ratios (finviz.com) website to look further into the numbers:

- 12 month trailing (current) P/E is 6.18
- EPS growth rate this year = 50%, next year 383%, next five years = 11%
- By Definition = P/E < EPS Growth Rate, 6.18 < 50
- The 52 week low was 10.22, the stock was trading at 16.94 range, 52 week high was 35.42 (accurate as of June 2020) meaning it's inside the range, but still undervalued.
- Current P/E = 6.18, Industry Average = 6.06, S&P = 19.84
- PEG Ratio = .55
- Earnings – Beat earnings three of previous four quarters, while badly missing earnings in March of 2020 by 162%
- Next four quarters EPS projections are much higher.

This fit most of my criteria, which is great. Let's take a look at the stock chart in Yahoo Finance for another view before we move forward and declare victory. See the massive movement down from their historical average in March 2020. If the company can rebound, it presents a massive opportunity at buying a stock at a bargain.

Ally Financial (ALLY) 5 year stock performance

According to the chart, the stock took a massive hit, over 50% loss in the stock price. Here's the great news. We know a few things based on the preliminary research. We know the stock was trending upwards since mid-2016, it had a high point of 35 dollars per share, and most notably, we know what caused the drop in the stock price (badly missing earnings). If the stock returns to normal performance, it represents 100% upside to the former stock price. This represents a potential great time to enter or scale into the stock ALLY, but obviously depends on the investment strategy.

The numbers don't lie as the stock is coming up by definition as a value stock. Value stocks will generally have some earnings misses, but keep in mind its analysts' projections of the company, not the company's internal projections. When a company misses earnings (more common with value stocks), their stock price is generally reflected the following day if not over the next few weeks after the earnings announcement. Like the example above with ALLY, this will result in a downward correction for the stock price. The size of the company (market capitalization) and the size of the miss (how many cents the estimate is off) will determine how much the stock pulls back.

What else could cause a significant drop in the stock? Well, there could be something cyclical going on, like seasonality of sales or if the company hasn't developed a new product or version in a highly competitive marketplace. This is the reason phone manufacturers like Apple (AAPL) or Samsung consistently develop new phones to replace aging products to generate new sales. There's also events beyond the control of the company. For example, in recent history, such as COVID-19 in March 2020, the majority of the stock market experienced a sell off. This is an example of an extraordinary event. Here's another idea that could happen.

Let's use potato chips as a product example and specifically Pepsi (PEP), who owns the Lays' potato chip manufacturing. If Lays' farmers crops were suddenly hit with a flurry of tornadoes that wiped out a ¼ of the supply of potatoes, it would be highly detrimental to the supply and prices that might rapid change to meet the demand curve. This is also true if something like disease spreads through growing crops resulting in higher prices due to a lower projected supply. The company couldn't suddenly raise its prices at the grocery store because of competitive balance, but it would likely sacrifice profits to keep prices at a stable level.

Remember the housing crisis in 2007 when the market had a complete downturn? Companies like Pepsi (PEP) that had no real capital interest in the housing or financial markets, still felt the full impact with a massive stock decline. The housing market caused the entire stock market and capital markets to collapse. These events have happened and will continue to happen in the future. The overall point is these global events impact all stocks and to be aware of them. **Hey, I thought you said value had less risk?** Yes, I did say that, but these things could happen to any industry or the overall marketplace, which could impact the portfolio.

Value investors generally wait for full valuation and also when the P/E expands naturally. P/E expands naturally when a stable company returns to form, has good earnings prospects, and outperforms its P/E by outperforming the growth expectations. If a stock has a P/E of 10 and a growth rate of 15, the price of the stock should grow by at least 15 percent, and all things being equal, the P/E doesn't have to expand. If a stock's P/E at any time becomes greater than its growth rate, it's no longer a value stock. The valuation is as simple as that.

If the P/E did become greater than the growth rate, at that time, the **typical value investor would sell the stock** and begin to research another value position. However, investors that used a mixed approach (which I'll discuss), the strategy could be to just hold the stock if there is room for further projected growth. At that point, it's important to understand where the future growth comes from such as company news, market news or improved outlook, which could ultimately change the dynamic. This could translate it into a growth stock. If this approach gets too involved, just focus on understanding if the stock P/E is more or less than the growth rate. It's that easy to identify if the stock position is a value stock or by use the alternative approach with a stock screener.

GROWTH INVESTING

Growth investing sounds much more positive than value investing, doesn't it? Of course, we all want the investments we've chosen to grow. That's the point, right? Well, that's not why it's called growth investing. A typical growth investor is looking for companies with high growth rates, and are willing to pay much more for their growth prospects. By saying they are willing to pay more, it's more accurately described as paying more for the valuation of the company. Keep in mind growth investing carries more risk than value investing so with risk there's reward.

Typical growth investors are seeking 10-20% returns, or even higher. Most notably, they are willing to accept the increased risk associated with this strategy. One variable I'd like to point out is growth companies typically do not pay dividends. This is because they are more concerned with growing product lines and scaling their operations to pay dividends that require more research and development capital (R&D). Some common characteristics of a growth stock:

- High revenue growth rates – odds are the growth company is in a period where the product(s) is in the initial sales cycle and people are paying a premium for it. Each time the new iPhone hits the stores and people line up to pay a premium.

- Growth rate exceeds the P/E ratio (definition of a growth stock). Remember, P/E stands for Price to Earnings ratio

- Very high projected growth next 1-3 years – Future earnings is exactly what investors are paying the premium to earn that growth.

- Quarterly reporting beats earnings estimates – Growth companies will routinely surprise Wall Street and surpass their earnings estimates by multiples.

- EPS consistently constantly – quarter over quarter growth is another solid metric to define a growth stock. (Remember EPS is Earnings Per Share)

- New technology or new products – some type of game changing or industry changing technology. The type of technology that really separates a company from its competition can put it in the growth mode (think about iPhones or a Tesla).

- Higher premium than EPS – It's not out of the question for growth companies to pay 40 times their earnings for high projected future growth

Here's a few examples of growth companies. The Internet phenomenon in the 90s where stocks would go up 50% in a day or a week where any company with a .com suddenly shot up. More recently, from 2010-2020, the tech FANG stocks all propelled the stock market to new highs. The FAANG stocks consisted of Facebook, Apple, Netflix, and Google. These companies all had much higher growth rates, but paid off. Growth investing is excited because it's generally accompanied by something new, like technology or advances in industries. Many tech companies can operate with much smaller budgets because they can generate sales online without the need for brick and mortar retail stores.

What company is a great example at retail, but currently has very few brick and mortar stores? Amazon.com was a pioneer in their industry because of their extensive distribution networks. The distribution network, warehouses, and logistics were all required to execute their two-day shipping strategy. For 10+ years, Amazon consistently lost money because they remained in growth mode to build their long-term strategy with CEO Jeff Bezo's aggressive leadership approach. Aggressive management teams aim for higher growth rates, and won't settle for anything less, but need to able to execute. They demand products and services that separate themselves from their competition.

Another example of one of the best growth companies (possibly the number one of our lifetime) is Apple (AAPL). Apple had a tremendous run in the late 2000s and again in the 2010s, experiencing growth rates of 30-200% annually. The company held a very high constant P/E, consistently beating higher growth expectations becoming one of the biggest success stories ever in the history of the stock market. Despite having generated constant successful sales quarters, analysts kept revising their estimates to project record breaking sales. Eventually its expectations were so high that unfortunately, it had to return back to normal levels in 2013, followed by growth again. To get a true picture of Apple's growth cycle, let's take a moment to review their stock chart over the twenty year stretch 2000-2020. As you can tell, Apple's upward momentum was mostly a growth company.

Apple's (AAPL) 20-year Stock Chart

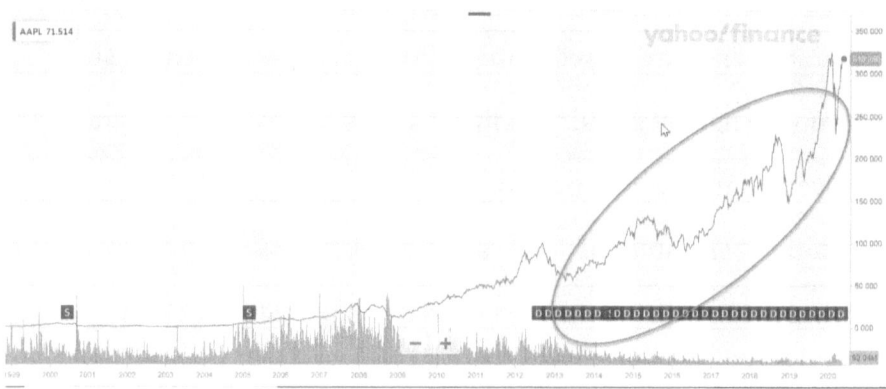

One last example of a high growth company to discuss in Pharmaceuticals is Intuitive Surgical (ISRG). High growth can be correlated to any industry, not just technology. Within the healthcare sector, new drugs are constantly in trials to be approved that could cure diseases and improve the condition of human life. Getting back to ISRG, the company manufacturers da Vinci surgical systems that allows doctors to performs surgeries using a robot. The surgery include areas gynecologic, urologic, general, cardiothoracic, and head and neck surgical procedures. This company is the leader by far in robotic surgery for patients, which promotes faster recovery and health among patients.

The company's products were some of the first accepted by the FDA, taking science fiction surgery (they claim) to reality. The company's innovative surgery robots, making surgery much less invasive, with better techniques, and speed up recovery vs. traditional recovery. After adoption started to take off, the company's stock price did as well with three large movements from 2007-2009, in the early 2010s and again in 2017-2019. See the chart below as an example of another stock that took time to mature, but the growth minded company with innovative technology, was well worth the wait to earn those returns.

Intuitive Surgical (ISRG) 20-year Stock Chart

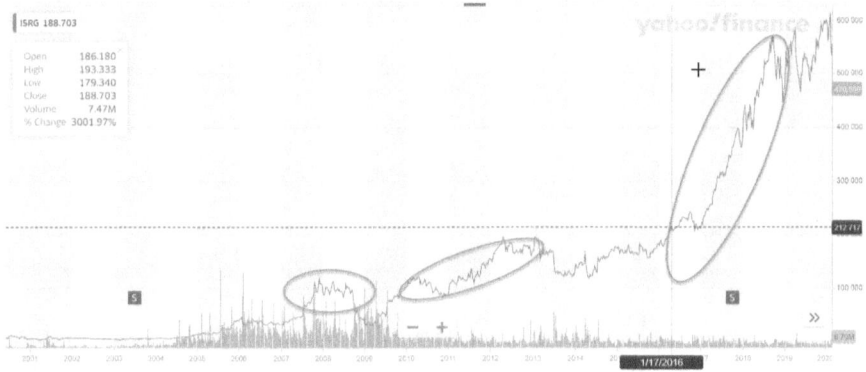

REMINDERS FOR GROWTH & VALUE INVESTING

To build a portfolio and scale into it (which is what I recommend), it takes time to build and maintain a quality portfolio. It doesn't matter if the investment strategy is geared towards either value or growth investing. Regardless of which style of investing preferred, here are some reminders for either style to keep in mind.

- Spread out assets – Allocate investment strategy by investing in multiple industries. Pick up different stocks across 5-10 industries to gather some diversification to have a stable portfolio of investments. This will lower risk.
- Don't watch the stock market channel every day! It will – IT WILL – drive you nuts, trust me on this. It doesn't do any good to constantly watch it.
- Check the portfolio at least once a quarter – That's only four times a year! That's it. Only four times a year. Check if any investments have fallen out of favor to revisit why it was purchased in the first place.
  - This also ties into value investing rule number two: don't watch every day.

We talked about Mixed Investing, a combination of growth and value, a few pages back. Let's dive into that topic now and explore how a quality portfolio is built.

MIXED INVESTING

Mixed investing is just as it sounds. It's providing a mix of both growth and value investing. The reason most investors will end up here is because it provides balance by emphasizing diversification. This is where I advise to start and grow because it helps to further diversify the potential portfolio along with the other pieces we will put together. I know most people know what diversify means, but I'd like to take time to break it down a few steps further.

Diversifying the portfolio simply means having a well-adjusted balance of investments. Earlier in the book, I broke down different capitalizations as well as value vs. growth investment options. This was to provide a general understanding of the investment options and how they are separated. As a quick refresher, here are the categories in which most investments are placed:

- Small Cap Growth
- Small Cap Value

- Mid-Cap Growth
- Mid-Cap Value
- Large Cap Growth
- Large Cap Value

Each of these is called an investment class. Remember the training earlier: the small cap growth type would be defined as an investment that has a market capitalization of $150 million - $1.5 billion and is projected for 15-20% growth (because its small cap). On the flip side, small cap value has the same market capitalization and stock price but is characterized as undervalued (falling short of expectations, P/E is lower than expected EPS growth). This is how most investment products / choices (stocks, ETFs, mutual funds) will appear when they are characterized.

This section is meant to bring up the importance of having a diverse portfolio with investments from each sector. It's really difficult to predict the company or sector that will outperform with the next big product, or simply beat their earnings. This is why I'm emphasizing the need to diversify the portfolio. The sectors within the stock market fall in and out of favor based on the reasons outlined earlier (analyst revisions, industry news, etc.). The more sectors owned, the greater chance for a balanced portfolio.

What's the right amount to keep invested? What's the right amount to keep in cash? These decisions will come down to each investor's discretion. My rule of thumb, it's I always like to have a small portion of cash on the sidelines (dependent on the market environment). This is in the case a stock I'm following takes a dip and I'd like to invest more. The portion of cash completely depends on the investor. I like to keep 5%-10% of my overall portfolio to maintain in cash. I'll reinforce this message in the sample portfolio section to help remember this concept. If starting with $10,000 in a portfolio, that means keeping $500-$1,000 to have ready in case an investment dips and opens a buying opportunity. Remember, money sitting in a brokerage account must rest inside a Money Market account.

Brokerage accounts work different than a checking account and as a result non-invested money must be kept in a Money Market Fund that can easily be liquidated. The amount of money to have on the sidelines naturally changes as investors age, the portfolio changes, and the money may be needed to subsidize income. OK, enough heavy lifting for a bit, let's transition to why investing is important and why having diversity in across assets is essential to the investment strategy.

To demonstrate this, let's revisit our example pair of friends from earlier, Larry & Charlie. Remember that Charlie was the better student and began investing earlier on in life (early 20s), and Larry waited till he was 30 years old to begin investing. Charlie and Larry went out to lunch and were having a discussion around the same time, Charlie began investing. Here's the following exchange:

Charlie – "Hey Larry, I was reading up on this investment stuff again."

Larry – "Oh gosh, here we go again with this investment stuff. Do you ever give it a rest?"

Charlie – "Well, I was reading something that I wanted to share about diversity in the investment strategy that should be used."

Larry – "Diversity is like people from different cultures, right? What does that have to do with investment strategy?"

Charlie – "I mean diversify, but it's kind of the same concept. It said that investors need to diversify their investments to spread out potential risk."

Larry – "I guess that makes sense, but I'll elect to keep my money in the bank account where I know it's safe without any risk."

Charlie – "OK, I'll let you know if I find out more…"

So here's another classic exchange between Larry and Charlie regarding investing. Charlie is clearly open to learning something new and Larry is acting closed minded to the idea of investing. Remember, it was Charlie who read the investment books and decided to try out the strategy of investing money early? It was also Charlie who invested far less, but ended up with a larger amount later in life. Well, now Charlie was putting into practice the next lesson he had studied which was on diversification. Charlie decided to spread out his money into five different stocks that he chose from companies he knew about that covered different capitalization caps and sectors. Charlie bought:

- Investment A – Small cap growth stock
- Investment B – Large cap value stock

- Investment C – Mid cap value stock

- Investment D – Mid cap growth stock

- Investment E – Small cap growth stock

While Charlie was investing in different types of stocks, Larry held to his word and kept his money in his savings account. After three years of leaving the stocks in the portfolio, and not selling or making adjustments (and allowing any dividends to reinvest), here are the returns per stock that he earned so he could follow-up his conversation with Larry. Charlie took out a sheet of paper and wrote down what happened with each investment for him to review with his good friend Larry when they met later on in the day. Charlie's investments turned out just fine. He had three stocks that were up, and two that were down.

- Investment A – Small cap growth stock – Increase ROI (Return On Investment) + 176%

- Investment B – Large cap value stock – Increase ROI +30%

- Investment C – Mid cap value stock – Decrease ROI – 12%

- Investment D – Mid cap growth stock – Decrease ROI – 80%
- Investment E – Small cap growth stock – Increase ROI +72%

As Charlie was eager to share what happened with his stocks, he met with Larry to talk about it. He had the investment analysis on what happened with his investments to make a comparison against the traditional bank account method that Larry stuck his money in. Larry, of course, never being shy about giving his opinion, was beaming that the savings account hadn't lost any money and had even gained a little bit.

Charlie – "Hey Larry, remember those stocks I bought a few years ago. Well, guess what, Larry? I got the results back."

Larry – "Oh yeah? Tell me what happened. How much money did you lose?"

Charlie – "Well, it's a bag of mixed results. I had three stocks that were up, and two that were down. There was one that was down 80%! I couldn't believe it."

Larry – "I told you not to invest in that crazy, risky stock market. I kept my money in my savings account and it went up a little bit. I think I got back like $15, but I didn't lose any."

Charlie – "Only $15?"

Larry – "Yeah, but remember, I didn't lose anything."

Charlie – "I ended up with a lot more than that."

Larry – "But I thought you said you lost like 80% on one investment?"

Charlie – "Yeah, I did, but the overall results are much better than $15."

Larry – "How in the world could you have done better? I didn't lose anything!"

Charlie – "Let me show you exactly what happened."

Larry was perplexed. He had gone the very safe route by leaving his money in his savings account and even made a few extra dollars. Charlie had lost 80% on one investment, yet he had still done better. This didn't make any sense to Larry. Let's go one step further into Charlie's investments. Charlie had investments that were both up and down that totaled into something much better than the $15 Larry received using the safe savings account. Clearly the mid-cap sector had rotated out of favor with the current market since that sector was down. The combined ROI for all five investments was 37.2% (Keep in mind I'm not discounting back with time value of money to keep the examples easy). How is this calculated? Well, take the ROI and multiply it by the initial investment to determine the actual number gain. Charlie invested $200 in each position for a total of $1,000 invested.

- Investment A – Increase ROI + 176% x $200 = $352
- Investment B – Increase ROI + 30% x $200 = $60
- Investment C – Decrease ROI – 12% x $200 = -$24
- Investment D – Decrease ROI – 80% x $200 = -$160
- Investment E – Increase ROI+ 72% x $200 = $144
- Total Return = $372
- ROI = Return / Initial Investment, $372 / $1,000 = 37.2%

Charlie's portfolio yielded just over $370 over a three year span, which is about a 12.4% return each year (yes I know I didn't discount it back, but let's keep the example easier to understand). An example like this highlights the necessity to diversify the portfolio as mentioned before. As stated earlier, it's never known which sector or industry will fall out of favor in the market. Take a minute to review the numbers and percentages above again. What other important takeaways can be derived from the above example using the results?

- Small cap growth stocks clearly outperformed the market (returns of +176% and +72%)

- Large cap value stocks performed to the market average (return of 30% over three years = average return of +10%)
  - This is consistent with overall history and average return of the stock market

- Mid-cap stocks underperformed significantly (returns of -80% and -12%)
  - These stocks could both be viewed as value stocks now since they are underperforming for three years in a row. This could be a buying opportunity now with that excess cash on the sideline we talked about earlier.

- If Charlie was a next level investor, he could have used a sell stop to limit the 80% loss to a much more reasonable rate – 15-20% loss for example.

○   This would have greatly increased the overall ROI for the portfolio.

Charlie's balanced portfolio shows what a well-diversified portfolio will accomplish. It should contain both growth potential and undervalued companies. The undervalued companies are ones that will hopefully return to form at some point, else they should be sold. The large cap stocks likely provide stability of paying dividends regularly (keeping in mind that most mature companies pay dividends, especially value stocks). The regular dividends can serve as a cash flow instrument to help grow the portfolio by reinvesting frequently. This adds yet another level of stability in the portfolio with easier to calculate returns. Beyond the stable companies, Charlie's portfolio demonstrated the excitement of growth companies as well as stability.

The example should help provide a better understanding about the different market caps and a balanced portfolio. Beyond key fundamentals, the next question begs, why care about them, why is it important, and how can it help? Most people have a psychological preference to large, middle, or small caps, whether they know it or not. Let me make an analogy with ask some questions. Answer the following questions and keep the answers written down. Think of the last time gambling or playing cards.

- Did you prefer risk or safety?

- If safety was 1 and risk was 10, where would you rank?

- Did you take $200 or $2,000, or even more to the casino?

- Were you an aggressive player or did you play conservative?

- Did you immediately pull money out of the ATM if you lost it?

- If you didn't go to the casino, you may just be risk adverse

- Is it more satisfying to not lose money than to win money?

Odds are these questions can provide some insight to handling risk. I'm not going to bend the truth, there is risk associated with investing in the stock market. The risk in the stock market can be managed. Keep in mind, there's risk of leaving money in a bank account. There's risk of not earning anything or very little in a checking or savings account. Large cap sectors and ETFs offer far less risk for a portfolio with more stability. On the flip side, small & micro-cap companies offer higher growth potential due to their inherent risk with preliminary growth stages. Apple (AAPL) was once a small cap company, and look at it today. It is one of the highest market capitalizations in the world. It can easily be reviewed using <u>Yahoo Finance with the stock symbol and locate Market cap</u>. We've spent quite a bit of time on market caps, let's transition to the execution of building a portfolio.

IMPLEMENTING A TARGET ASSET ALLOCATION

Implementing a target asset allocation within a portfolio consists of a diverse mix of investments to survive the ebbs and flows of the market. The market is like the ocean; it moves up and down constantly every day, every month, and every year. Having a diverse portfolio from different sectors and market caps is essential to growing a portfolio that will keep gains and minimize potential losses from the stock market over a period of time. In the following section, there's some recommended mock portfolios that can be used as an initial starting point.

The portfolio you start out using will certainly not be the same that as folks approach retirement. Remember, it's just a starting point and should be adjusted accordingly at times. Some of the stocks selected will ultimately end up huge winners, some will be average, and of course some will be down. Lastly, there will also be some that aren't picked up and turn into huge returns and you'll want to kick yourself (but you won't). It's important to stay the course, continue with the strategy, and don't panic during the rough times.

As a general rule of thumb, remember that the stock market is up two out of every three years (that's a pretty good ratio) and has been up 11% overall in over 100 years. Keep in mind, stocks will fluctuate and will go down many times throughout the course of a year. Don't allow those stocks to get in the way of the investment strategy. Sometimes those technological advances will give the portfolio a nice boost and sometimes make up the entire ROI.

Remember those risk questions about risk and casino habits I asked earlier? Depending on how the questions were answered should influence the level of risk you are willing to accept, and will help decide how to invest money with specific target allocations. This section should provide a solid foundation for years to come and should be altered accordingly depending on a few factors like risk tolerance, age, and expected retirement age. There will be an aggressive, conservative, and a mixed portfolio to look over, so please use them as guidance to decide which is closest aligned to your investment style. Remember, it's your money and your decisions.

HEADS UP BOOK CHANGES AHEAD

One last disclosure based on the re-write as my second edition regarding portfolio performance. My first edition also had mock portfolios that have now all been adjusted to reflect my thoughts on the next 5-10 years and how to position risk and reward. As a quick moment of reflection to provide full visibility and insight into how my mock portfolios from 2015 (the Old Mock Portfolios with positions can be found in Chapter 13), here are the results:

- Conservative approach with 15 positions, 86% ROI in 5 years

- Moderate approach with 15 positions, 107% ROI in 5 years

- Aggressive approach with 15 positions, 102% ROI in 5 years

Something I'd like to point out is these investment portfolios don't take into account getting out of the position with major drops or changes. They reflect only if the investor initially purchased equal amounts at the starting point with no additional changes to the positions, no changes to the amount invested, and reinvest all the dividends. These are important variables when comparing the results with any other portfolio for like to like comparison. After this side story, we'll go over the new mock portfolios I've created.

Side Story #4 – Back in 2004, there was a company that was just about to file for its IPO (Initial Public Offering) and I had a strong sense that it would do well. My reasons were none more that I used the service on a daily basis. Many folks that I knew also used it, but I had no idea how it made money. That last part really bugged me. I went to my Dad and told him, "I'd like to take $10,000 in my portfolio in and invest in this company, what do you think?" Neither of us knew what would happen with the company, but I just said I believed in the product and many others loved their service. Ultimately, since neither of us could answer how they made money, I decided to not invest into it. Google (GOOG) took off, and almost 10 years later, the stock went over $1,000 per share from the IPO around $100, 10x the value. I tell this story in hopes that it will help you one day when it happens to you. It's one of my *big investment regrets, but I can't let it bother me because I have had others that have doubled, tripled, and done extremely well. This will happen to you. The key is to not let it bother you and stick to the rest of the investment strategy.*

SAMPLE PORTFOLIOS

In the next few pages, I've laid out some sample portfolios that can utilized to get started. Keep in mind it's your money and no one knows your personal tolerance for risk. Once reviewing the sample portfolios, it should be apparent that all the portfolios begin with a large allocation towards The Fort. The Fort is the foundation (consisting of 4-6 ETFs) for any portfolio that won't require constant maintenance and will allow an easier "hands off" approach. The Fort will help weather the ups and downs of the stock market by providing the required stability and safety to grow an effective portfolio. The biggest difference between the three sample portfolios regarding the foundation is the different allocations within The Fort. Since The Fort offers the most stability, it's easy to imagine that it would be higher with a conservative portfolio and lower with a more aggressive portfolio. I would recommend starting any type of portfolio with a foundation of The Fort. I advise adding to it until it comprises of 20%-50% of the portfolio. Monthly investment allocation in a brokerage account is my preferred method to build the portfolio.

Before we jump right in, there's something missing from all three sample portfolios that I'd like to point out. All three are lacking some key elements such as how much to keep in cash reserves, percentage to allocate to bonds, and investment frequency. Let me first discuss the cash perspective. Earlier, I mentioned keeping some cash on the side in case a new investment opportunity comes up or a favorite investments dips on specific news (misses earnings, analyst revision). I still recommend keeping 5-10% of cash in reserve for situations like this. For example, if the total portfolio is $10,000, then keeping $500-$1,000 in reserve is ideal. *This is just a simple recommendation whereas each investor should make that decision based on right amount or right percentage for the portfolio*.

The next missing piece is bond allocation. As a refresher, a bonds is a loan, with the investor as the lender and company/government as lender. Bonds offer a much clearer indication of the potential return as the details are provided on the issue. The issuer of the bond, which can be a government entity or business, promises to pay the money back when the bond matures and comes due. Bonds are generally recommended as a fixed income product when people approach retirement because they cannot afford to risk any loss of principal (principal is the initial investment).

As investors advance beyond the age of 40, a portion of their portfolio should be allocated to fixed income products like bonds. After 40, 10% of the portfolio should contain fixed income and upwards of 50% when reaching the age of 55-70. Please take a note of that range from 10-50% and the corresponding age ranges. This is completely dependent upon tolerance for risk. Fixed income products are less risky than stocks and provide a very stable ROI. I included a bond fund that has a tremendous track record on each of the sample portfolios for substituting for age requirements. The bond fund symbol is located in the bottom paragraph of each sample portfolio. For more help with bonds, check out a book I recommend in the extra information in Chapter 13.

The last piece missing from the sample portfolio section is frequency of investing. This is completely dependent upon certain factors such as age, amount to invest, and free cash flow. There are a few different ways to approach this on how to fund and build your portfolio. Below are some sample portfolios to provide direction, but it might take time to create it. Remember earlier the different scenarios of folks saving for something (retirement, a new car, paying off debt)? In those examples there were different strategies incorporated to provide realistic situations.

I recommend using the same strategy for investing equivalent to paying monthly bills. Start by simply paying yourself a specific amount each month. I've talked about Fidelity and their platform several times. Using the mobile app, it's possible to do this at a very reasonable cost. Given the brokerage investment community has moved to $0 trading costs, I view this is an excellent strategy to get started.

If you're like me and had a lump sum, but still wanted to scale into an investment, here's what I recommend. Let's say I want to have a portfolio of $10,000. I would use a mock portfolio listed below, scale into the portfolio with monthly investments of $1,000 monthly for 10 months. This would reduce my risk and provide flexibility along the way. It's less scary, I would learn along the way, and would get in the habit of investing monthly. Remember, these are simply sample portfolios and every investor must make their own investment decisions. Regardless if any of the strategies, make sure to elect Full Dividend Reinvestment to capture the full effect and impact of compound interest.

These are sample portfolios and based everything we learned so far, each investor should assess their own risk tolerance and financial situation. I've provided a few different strategies above to help get started; however, if you do have outstanding debt (credit card, student loans, or car loan) at high interest rates, it may be wiser to pay off that debt first. Paying off debt with a guaranteed return, is smarter in the short term until it's paid off in full.

POTENTIAL PORTFOLIO ALLOCATION ONE (CONSERVATIVE)

IJR – Fidelity Small Cap Mixed ETF

IVV – Fidelity Large Cap Mixed ETF

IJJ – Fidelity Mid Cap Value ETF

ITOT – iShares Total Market Index ETF

FNCL – Fidelity Financial ETF

SQ – Square – offers digital financial solutions, starting to integrate into

ROK – Rockwell Automation – offers architecture, software, and automation solutions

NEE – NextEra Energy – Smart energy company that sells power in North America

WTR – Aqua America – One of the largest water utility companies in the Northeastern U.S.

AMZN – Amazon.com – Industry leader in selling retail products

V – Visa – Global payments technology company connecting business to consumers

CLX – Clorox – manufacturers and markets consumer products (cleaning, household, lifestyle)

KR – Kroger's Grocery – retailer of supermarket goods (food, essentials, etc)

DIS – Disney – Global entertainment brand including theme parks, merchandise, and content

CGNX – Cognex – provides machine vision products for automation support in manufacturing

The first sample portfolio consists of various sectors and market segments. Most notably the portfolio concentrates heavier on The Fort with 5 ETFs that cover most all major market caps (small, medium, large, and mega) to provide high stability. I would recommend having at least 50% of the portfolio dedicated to 5 ETFs with 10% allocation towards each ETF, then using a simplistic 5% allocation towards each of the other 10 investments. The rest of the selections stretch across industries consisting of Large and Mid-Cap companies that concentrate with mixed and value selections. These will provide a steady stream of dividends, stable growth, and low exposure to risk.

The sectors involved consist of utilities (both electric and water), retail and consumer goods as consumer staples (Amazon, Clorox & Kroger), financial services with exposure to cryptocurrency (Square), everyday consumer expenses and products (Visa, and Disney) and some calculated growth opportunities through automation (Rockwell and Cognex). This type of portfolio will allow the type of "leave it alone and let it grow" investment strategy that will keep investors concentrating on their day job without having to worry.

If over the age of 40, consider adding a fixed income product to the portfolio and replacing some of the risk in the sample portfolio (ROK & CGNX) with discretion. For a recommendation, check out Harbor Fund's Bond Fund (HADBX), it has a very steady track record, posting consistent returns with bond payments (3% bond yield) the last ten years. Its management team has generated returns routinely and sticks to their long engrained winning strategies. Again, if over the age of 40, please consider having fixed income in the portfolio to protect the hard earned principal. What percentage? That answer is up to each investor dependent on age as I touched on a recommended percentage of 10% at 40 years of age and increase it with age.

POTENTIAL PORTFOLIO ALLOCATION TWO (AGGRESSIVE)

IJR – Fidelity Small Cap Mixed ETF

IJK – Fidelity Mid Cap Growth ETF

ROM – Ultra Technology ETF

ALLY – Ally Financial – provides digital financial product and services

MANT – Mantech – provides cybersecurity solutions

VRNS – Varonis – provides cybersecurity solutions

SQ – Square – offers digital financial solutions, starting to integrate into

ROK – Rockwell Automation – offers architecture, software, and automation solutions

ADSK – Autodesk – builds information systems for workflow solutions for businesses

ATVI – Activision – creates and sells online gaming, video gaming consoles

BRKS – Brooks Automation – provides automation and artificial intelligence solutions

CGNX – Cognex – provides machine vision products for automation support in manufacturing

INVE – Identiv – provides security solutions

DIS – Disney – Global entertainment brand including theme parks, merchandise, and content

SGMO – Sangamo – biotechnology company that focuses on genetics using gene therapy

Portfolio Two, the aggressive profile, as you may have guessed, has significant more upside and risk associated with the sample portfolio. The first thing I need to point out is to reduce the allocation towards The Fort. There's only three ETFs included and I suggest 20-30% total allocated to them. As a point of reference, The Fort in the conservative portfolio was up to 50% allocation as the base of the portfolio. There's a much more growth oriented strategy with Cybersecurity and Security (VRNS, MANT, INVE), Automation (BRKS, CGNX, ROK) and online gaming (ATVI). Most notably, it's the first portfolio mentioning any bioscience with gene therapy exposure (SGMO). There's a usual staple (DIS), and financial exposure (SQ, ALLY) and a very aggressive technology focused ETF (ROM). The strategy is very focused on future growth and companies striving for newer technology within the marketplace.

Similar to the first sample portfolio, if over the age of 40, consider adding a fixed income product to the portfolio and replacing some of the sample portfolio with discretion. I'd consider the same fund from above, Harbor Fund's Bond Fund (HADBX).

POTENTIAL PORTFOLIO ALLOCATION THREE (MIXED)

IJT – Fidelity Small Cap Growth ETF

IVV – Fidelity Large Cap Mixed ETF

IJK – Fidelity Mid Cap Growth ETF

ITOT – iShares Total Market Index ETF

ALLY – Ally Financial – provides digital financial product and services

MANT – Mantech – provides cybersecurity solutions

VRNS – Varonis – provides cybersecurity solutions

WTRG – Essential Utilities – provides water utilities throughout the United States

SQ – Square – offers digital financial solutions, starting to integrate into

ROK – Rockwell Automation – offers architecture, software, and automation solutions

ADSK – Autodesk – builds information systems for workflow solutions for businesses

ATVI – Activision – creates and sells online gaming, video gaming consoles

CLX – Clorox – manufacturers and markets consumer products (cleaning, household, lifestyle)

CGNX – Cognex – provides machine vision products for automation support in manufacturing

INVE – Identiv – provides security solutions

Portfolio Three, the last portfolio listed here, is the mixed portfolio, which has the investment strategy one would expect consisting of both growth and value company types. The allocation of The Fort increases from the aggressive portfolio to 30-40%, down from 50% of the conservative portfolio. This shows the sliding scale of how much The Fort should be allocated in any given portfolio to have enough safety to sustain the ebs and flows of the stock market.

The portfolio provides growing financial services (SQ, ALLY), cybersecurity and security services (MANT, VRNS, INVE), automation (CGNX, ROK), online gaming/business services in a growth mode (ATVI, ADSK) and some utilities and consumer services to round it out (WTRG, CLX). This mock portfolio offers the most balance of risk and stability. I'm going to venture a guess that some of these names are pretty common with a mix of some their unknown. These are positive signs that should provide some confidence about the type of investor you are aiming to be with growing knowledge to move out of the beginner stage.

As a reminder, if over the age of 40, consider adding a fixed income product to the portfolio and replacing some of the sample portfolio with discretion. I'd consider the same fund from above,

Harbor Fund's Bond Fund (HADBX). Fixed income is a necessity to preserve the base principal of the portfolio as you age and cannot risk loss of principal.

The next section visits how I review different companies to make stock selections. I try to keep this a bit higher level for folks that may choose to use the stock screeners (like Yahoo and Finviz) to select their own portfolio.

Chapter Eleven

HOW I EVALUATE STOCKS WITH A SUMMARY TO TIE EVERYTHING TOGETHER

B elow is a quick synopsis of how I review stocks after using one of the three methods (Common Sense, Wall Street, ETF Breakdown). As far as frequency of review, I review my portfolio monthly and/or quarterly depending on the position and its volatility. I do this to understand if the companies I decided to invest in to determine if they still performing the same way I originally analyzed.

For example, if a stock is rated higher in risk and could be volatile with high growth potential, I tend to put Sell Stops (click here for the Appendix on how to) on those positions with a 25% trailing loss to limit potential downside. On the flip side, if the stock or ETF has a low beta (remember the risk indicator), tends to be conservative, and has slower growth rates, I wouldn't have to review it but maybe 1-2 times annually. Let's transition to the fundamental valuations I find important.

P/E VS. FORWARD P/E

As a reminder, P/E is Price to Earnings ratio. It measures a company's valuation at any given time by taking the current share price and dividing it over the last 12 months earnings per share (EPS). For example, Visa (V) in January 2015 was trading about 260 per share with a 12 month's EPS of 8.65, what is the P/E? 265/8.65 = 30.16. Remember, the P/E translates to if the company is characterized as growth or value vs. the growth rate. How does the future outlook stack up for the company? Is it in line with expectations, falling behind, or beating them? I personally like to see companies that are at least in line or beating analyst expectations because I want to see that future growth become reality when the P/E naturally expands (with the stock price). Future P/E and projections are what analysts are estimating for future growth. *Recommendation – Good evaluation metric across All Market Caps*

PEG – PRICE/EARNINGS GROWTH RATIO

This formula calculates how much more or less an investor is paying for a particular stock. It's pretty easy. Take the current P/E ratio and divide it over the 5-year EPS growth rate. If the value is over 1.0, the security is fairly valued and likewise if it's under 1.0 the market isn't fully valuing the future growth. Let's stick with Visa (V) which had a PEG of 1.81 in January 2015. This means Visa is valued fairly according the PEG of 1.81. As a friendly reminder, the PEG can be found and used in the stock screeners. This PEG tells the investor they are paying premium to purchase Visa and there could better deals out there. *Recommendation – Best if used when evaluating Large Cap & Mid-Cap stocks*

QUICK & CURRENT RATIO

Both of these are indicators of how much cash flow the company is sitting on vs. the long term debt that is owed. These ratios have strong dependencies on the industry and market capitalization (large cap value vs. small cap growth). Small cap growth companies generally have more debt because they are growing at much higher rates, whereas large cap mature companies will carry far less debt according to their cash. Ideally, I like to see the ratios over 1.0 at least (more cash than debt), but will sacrifice to less than 1.0 if it's an emerging company with newer technology or small cap company. Understanding why the company has lots of debt is important to not rule out a potential great idea since debt can be used for many purposes. ***Recommendation – Good metrics to use on All Market Caps***

RETURN ON EQUITY (ROE) RATIO

This ratio looks at how much profit companies generate with shareholder money to get a true ROE. It's a ratio that should be important to shareholders because it reviews what the company is doing with their capital investment. The ratio is related to company profitability as a whole, and I like to see this as another gauge in the industry leaders. This is a ratio to learn since it directly impacts the investor. ***Recommendation – Best used for Large Cap & Mid-Cap***

INVENTORY TURNOVER

This is especially important for companies that manufacture, distribute, and sell physical goods (retail or distributors). Take

Coca-Cola (KO) for example. It's an important ratio to understand how often Coca-Cola turns over its products (sold and replaced) in a specific period, which is generally 30 days as a standard. If Coca-Cola is selling its' products in less period of time, that's great for investors. Remember, the higher the inventory rate, the higher the turnover, the better it is for physical goods. ***Recommendation – Best used for Large Cap & Mid-Cap***

OPERATING & PROFIT MARGIN

I'm very interested in these percentages because it tells exactly how much the company is making per product sold. I also really like to know how it stacks up against the industry and would be willing to accept lower thresholds for larger companies because of stability with mature product lines. More stability equates to fewer new products emerging into the marketplace. The reverse can be said about new products for small cap companies because they produce much higher margins as their products are much earlier in the life cycle. Those products reward companies with top dollar ROI because of the newness of the product. Remember the Product Life Cycle we discussed earlier? A few examples that fit into this model would be the early Apple iPhone and the all-electric cars Tesla manufacturers. Early on in the life cycle, products tend to sell for a more expensive price whereas prices tend to drop over time to attract more consumers. ***Recommendation – Use on All Market Caps***

PROFIT MARGIN VS. THE INDUSTRY AVERAGE

Similar to the above ratio, this average looks at a company's profit margin vs. the overall industry it is in. For example, Visa in Q4 of 2014 had a gross profit margin of 65%. Is this good or bad? It's outperforming the industry average, meaning it makes more money than competitors. That's a great statistic to look for. I like to see how the company is performing vs. the industry average to get a gauge of how to read some of the data. This is essential for large cap companies to make sure they are leading their competitors or are in the top 15%. If the profit margin is better than the industry, the stock price has a better opportunity to lead its peers. ***Recommendation – Best used for Large Cap & Mid-Cap***

DIVIDEND YIELD

This could be important whenever evaluating mature companies because it will project very close to what's expected for potential return on investment (ROI). The yield plus last year's growth rate can tell if it's going to potentially be between a 12-15% return or a 15-20% return. Most large and mega cap companies pay dividends. In general, dividend payouts are very consistent and as they continue to be increased over time, providing even more transparency about the potential ROI. *Recommendation – Best used for Large Cap & Mid-Cap*

EPS GROWTH (NEXT 3-5 YEARS)

When it comes to growth companies, this is a very important data point. Something I'd like to point out is company's stock price will be adjusted based on future projections and guidance from the company and analysts covering the company. Earnings Per Share growth is a key indicator for all companies characterized as a growth company because when the EPS grows, shares will be worth more. It's as simple as that. The EPS growth rate will show what the company expects to growth by within the next 3-5 years. If the growth is in line or above expectations, the investor will be rewarded with a higher stock price. I mentioned Telsa (TSLA) earlier as a growth stock, its' projected EPS growth in 2016 is over 360%. That's the growth investors are paying for, along with its' future growth projections. The rates differ across different industries, but if using a stock screener, it can quickly find companies growing at different rates dependent upon preference. ***Recommendation – Use on All Market Caps***

COMPETITION

Checking out a company's competition to have valuations to compare against, is a smart technique for analysis. A very easy way to do this is to us finance.google.com, type in the symbol or company name, and search. Once the selection comes up, there will be similar companies in the industry listed below the stock chart. For example, if I searched Tesla (TSLA), I would find Porsche, Audi, Toyota, and Ford as related companies in the same industry. I could then compare the financial numbers for Tesla and Audi to understand

their competition. ***Recommendation – Best used for Large Cap &***
Mid-Cap

MACRO ENVIRONMENT

The last piece that should be reviewed is understanding the macro environment. This is a general gauge about what's going on in the domestic U.S. and international economy that could possibly affect the portfolio. I'm not saying go out and study the macro environment, but have an idea of what's going on. In late 2014 and early 2015, the price of oil plummeted from over $100 a barrel to $50 a barrel. In 2019, it plummeted to less than $20 per barrel. Why is this important? This means if owning oil stocks, they could possibly be down in the portfolio rather quickly. This may have hit the sell stop and trigged the sale. Many world events affect the stock market and individual stocks like the price of oil, the U.S. Presidential Election, a war, or even Christmas time (most retail companies estimate 40% of their sales around Christmas). COVID-19 (Coronavirus) changed the world in 2020 with people not traveling (airline & hotel industries plummeted), very few car sales, people ordering most groceries online (AMZN, GRUB, and most employees were working from home (think Video Conferencing – ZOOM) among others. Think about how any of these could possibly affect the portfolio to stay on top of trends. It could just save a few bucks by spotting an early trend. *Recommendation – Use on All Market Caps*

UNDERSTAND HOW THE COMPANY MAKES MONEY

One takeaway I've pointed out in the book several times is I always like to know what the company does and how it generates cash flow. This is a very easy and important thing to understand with some easy investigation on the internet. By understanding their business model, it will be easier to notice a potential upswing or downswing within the company or sector. Let me give an example. Remember when Microsoft (MSFT) debuted Windows Vista back in 2007? The product had several bugs that it eventually led Microsoft to pull Vista from store shelves. If owning Microsoft at the time, it may be easier to identify before announced earnings that the new product was a disaster. A simple Google Finance search for the company or symbol can provide this information at a high level without digging too deep. ***Recommendation – Use on All Market Caps***

Those are the main things I like to look for when researching or comparing potential investments for my portfolio. It's not incredibly difficult or at least it shouldn't sound like it as that was my intent. Just like anything new, it takes time and practice getting adjusted to trying something new. The best advice I can give is to try putting some of this information into use. Perform a dry run, research a company, any company. Don't be afraid because of all the reasons I explained throughout the book. As an example, if I wanted to research Proctor & Gamble (PG), I would simply type in PG in Google Finance. To get a snapshot about what's going on with the company, there's a news panel on the right hand side. This grabs the latest headlines of the company to quickly understand if there's a new product, how earnings have been, or if there's something wrong. It's quite useful. Go do this, and see how much information you started to understand at analyzing stocks.

Chapter Twelve

10 THINGS TO REMEMBER

As we are nearing the conclusion of the book, I'd like to leave a summary of everything that's I've taught and hopefully you have learned. The best way to revisit this book, is to look review a summary of the book in 2-3 pages that can serve as a powerful reminder, instead of re-reading the entire book. I compacted it down into a "10 things to remember" section that is all about making people better investors and helping meet their financial goals. Remember to go back through this section and the "how to evaluate stocks" section to serve as a guide and faster review.

1. TOO HARD TO BEAT INFLATION

Simply put, it's really challenging to beat inflation by leaving money in a savings account. Inflation comes in many different forms and eats into the annual salary. It's not the amount that's earned that's crucial because it's more important to know the percentage by which inflation will impact us all. Look at a savings account that yields .5%, the stock market that has historically (over 100 years) provided a ROI of 11%, and average inflation percentage of -3.5%. That's when the numbers really begin to tell the story and should help guide decisions.

2. INFLATION COMES IN MANY FORMS

Remember all the other angles of inflation besides milks, eggs, and bread. Keep in mind other major expenses like the cost of cars, gas, houses, and college tuition. When the government tells consumers that the average inflation is extremely low, it doesn't take into account all the other purchases necessary that occur in life. Don't let the CPI (Consumer Price Index) lie about inflation. You are a much smarter consumer than that.

3. THE EARLIER START, THE BETTER — REMEMBER LARRY VS. CHARLIE

Charlie started much earlier with a really small amount of $1,000 earlier in life. Larry started with double that amount ($2,000) 10 years later, but Charlie still ended with a bigger amount. The earlier start with investing, the greater the amount will grow to be with compound interest and the time value of money principals I taught earlier.

4. COMPOUND INTEREST AND THE RULE OF 72

Speaking of compound interest, this is another critical concept. Remember what Albert Einstein said all those years ago about the magic of compound interest being the 8th greatest wonder of the world? He wasn't lying. By letting investments remain investments and not become more expenses, they can build wealth. The interest earned will compound on top of principal and interest, making the investment grow rapidly. The Rule of 72, remember that one? Take the ROI from the entire portfolio and divide by 72. This will tell exactly how long it will take for those funds to double. Multiply it by two, and the investment will quadruple in value in that time frame.

5. PAY YOURSELF

Don't forget the simple principal of paying yourself by maintaining a budget and spending plan. I mean, every month you pay someone else (as in bills), right? Well, with the leftover cash do you ever think to pay yourself? Does it stay in the checking account or savings account earning .25% interest? Start to create a monthly budget in a different way, as it can make a major difference months and years later. Make a plan to set aside as little as a $50 payment into another account in a brokerage account and maintain the new habit. Perhaps the concept to pay yourself will take some time, but after a few months, it will become second nature.

6. THE FORT

The foundation for a house has the same level of importance as the foundation of a portfolio. That foundation is known as The Fort when it comes to setting up the stable base of the portfolio. The Fort (inclusive of 3-5 ETFs) will help weather the ups and downs of the stock market by providing the required stability and safety to grow an effective portfolio. The Fort will spread out enough allocation to several stocks that will reduce risk significantly. Not only does it reduce risk, but it reduces the need to constantly watch the portfolio. The ideal percentage allocation to The Fort is between 25 -50% of the total portfolio.

7. ALLOCATION SPREADS THE RISK

This goes directly into some of the ideas mentioned earlier with diversifying the portfolio to survive the ebbs and flows of the market. The market is like the ocean; it moves up and down constantly every day, every month, and every year. Having a diverse portfolio from different sectors and market capitalizations is essential to growing a strong portfolio to keep all those gains from investments over a period of time. Know the importance of having a diverse portfolio with different market caps to maintain a steady balance. There's never a need to get greedy and put all money into one stock. Remember those folks that got hit hard during the tech bubble or housing bubble. They got greedy. Learn from their mistakes.

8. HOW TO PICK A STOCK — YOU KNOW MORE THAN YOU THINK

(Common Sense vs. Wall Street Way vs. ETF Breakdown)

COMMON SENSE WAY

The next time a big purchase comes up, try and see who manufactures that product and identify the demand among your inner circle of family or friends. This happens all the time, and sometimes by simple observation, one can quickly see from the consumer point of view the latest trend happening right in from of you. After the observations, check the earnings report in Google Finance to see how they are doing. Remember that all these companies report earnings quarterly, meaning that while new products are out, the sales won't be reported until months later. You just may just find a great stock idea. For the more disciplined approach, use the Wall Street Way.

WALL STREET WAY

Using the Wall Street Way method to identify potential investments involves using a stock screener. A stock screener is an automated online tool used to match up the exact criteria selected to find the ideal stocks. Using this method also requires stock analysis using different ratios in accordance with what is trying to be accomplished. The types of stocks will vary when it comes to market capitalization, price, and growth, just to name a few factors. The best way to look for companies that accomplish the investment goals is to utilize a stock screener.

ETF BREAKDOWN

Using the ETF Breakdown Way means finding companies poised to break out that own a growing product or technology by breaking down an ETF. Breaking down the ETF is a process of recognizing an industry (technology, manufacturing), a trend (artificial intelligence, data analysis), or market segment (small cap growth), reviewing the companies that make up that ETF, and analyzing stocks to find opportunities to invest. That sounds like a lot, but it can be really worth it. Identifying themes include examples like Artificial Intelligence, Cyber Security, Robotics, and Life Science.

WIN SOME, LOSE SOME (DON'T LET IT BOTHER YOU)

Every year, most portfolios have winners and losers, some by a lot and some just barely. The overall balance (based on historical data) will yield a positive ROI and upwards direction. Keep in mind that every now and then there will be one really big investment regret. Remember this principal to not let it bother you and more importantly, learn from the mistakes (like my example with not investing with Google). Why? Because you'll have others that double and triple in ROI and do extremely well (trust me on this). This happened to me and it will 100% guaranteed happen to you at some point along the way. The key is to not let it bother you and to stick to the rest of the investment strategy. Short term losses can be utilized in tax strategy to reduce income taxes or taxes on gains and dividends.

IT'S A LONG TERM STRATEGY

I want to finish the book exactly how I started it. Investing should be viewed as a long term strategy that isn't a get rich quick scheme. It is something that you have now learned and understand the fundamental concepts of how the stock market works. I know at times it will make you nervous because the stock market goes up and down constantly, but I still have two words for you: DON'T WORRY!! I have lived through several down markets, and my portfolio is still afloat, and doing quite well. Remember to stick to the strategy. Regardless of market fluctuations, on average the stock market has returned 11%. Always remember that number.

I made several mentions of an extra chapter or index in the book. I included a bonus chapter after this section. The section is loaded with additional how-to's like place a stock order, types of ETFs, account types, further explanation about bonds, and some books that I found helpful along the way in my journey. The account types can be very helpful for avoiding probate for loved ones, or even setting up the right account for a child's college savings. At the very end, I included a list of key terms as well in case you need to research something I mentioned.

Thanks so much for sticking with me. There are a few things I want to note before we wrap up here at the end. If you found this book helpful to you and your future or present investment journey, please take the time to rate it on Amazon.com? Authors rely so heavily on ratings to help other readers get the same experience you did. Remember in the next few pages, I've included a few bonus sections below that go into a few more segments that will be needed along the way.

I truly hope that I helped you understand and form a solid foundation about investing to use for years to come. If you have any feedback or questions you'd like to send to me directly, my email is arichwagen23@gmail.com and twitter handle is @arichwagen23. Don't be shy, I promise I will reply. Happy and safe investing.

Alex Richwagen has been studying financial markets for over 20 years. He earned his Series 7 License from FINRA in 2013. Alex also earned his Master's Degree in Business Administration from the University of Central Florida in 2012 and is a certified Lean Six Sigma Black Belt. Alex gained a wealth of knowledge from his experience at Fortune 500 and Fortune 100 companies, which helps him understand the dynamics of Corporate America.

Alex has been independently helping others with their finances and investments for years. He wrote this book to relate the subject of investing to anybody and to truly help anyone willing to learn about financial markets and investing. Alex is the founder and CEO of Cornholeonwater Corp and resides in Clearwater, FL.

Chapter Thirteen

MORE BONUS MATERIAL TO HELP

HEADS UP BOOK CHANGES AHEAD

2015 BOOK PERFORMANCE

Please see the results of the mock portfolios. This is assuming the investor puts in equal amounts across each stock. For example, it's assumed the investor was trying to allocate equal shares (let's say $10,000 portfolio) and divided up $10,000 across the 14 positions. This also assumes the investor would remove any stocks that were bought out (DirecTV was bought by AT&T, or PetSmart that went private).

CONSERVATIVE MOCK PORTFOLIO RETURN — 86%

Symbol	Starting Price 2015	Ending Price Beg 2020	Return
VB	114.16	162.30	42%
VV	94.69	148.23	57%
VOE	87.31	117.20	34%
RFG	121.29	149.87	24%
VNQ	86.55	93.93	9%
VIG	78.42	125.37	60%
DUK	87.35	93.72	7%
WTR	26.59	50.57	90%
COST	143.32	304.68	113%
AMZN	290.74	1864.72	541%
GILD	102.21	62.98	-38%
V	65.13	193.77	198%
SAM	284.00	367.95	30%
PG	90.25	126.40	40%
Average			86%

AGGRESSIVE MOCK PORTFOLIO RETURN — 102%

Symbol	Starting Price 2015	Ending Price Beg 2020	Return
VB	114.16	162.30	42%
VV	94.69	148.23	57%
VOT	101.32	162.10	60%
RFG	121.29	149.87	24%

Symbol	Starting Price 2015	Ending Price Beg 2020	Return
ROM	37.82	171.25	353%
VIG	78.42	125.37	60%
QCOM	74.42	90.26	21%
TSLA	206.66	478.16	131%
WPRT	3.60	2.70	-25%
GILD	102.21	62.98	-38%
TWTR	40.17	32.78	-18%
FB	77.74	218.06	180%
ELY	8.13	21.40	163%
SHPG	209.00	179.20	-14%
ARWR	9.06	58.00	540%
Average			102%

MIXED MOCK PORTFOLIO RETURN — 107%

Symbol	Starting Price 2015	Ending Price Beg 2020	Return
VB	114.16	162.30	42%
VV	94.69	148.23	57%
VOT	101.32	162.10	60%
RFG	121.29	149.87	24%
ROM	37.82	171.25	353%
VIG	78.42	125.37	60%
V	65.13	193.77	198%
GILD	102.21	62.98	-38%
TWTR	40.17	32.78	-18%

Symbol	Starting Price 2015	Ending Price Beg 2020	Return
WTR	26.59	50.57	90%
COST	143.32	304.68	113%
AMZN	290.74	1864.72	541%
SAM	284.00	367.95	30%
DKS	53.54	48.25	-10%
Average			107%

TYPES OF ORDERS

There are two main types of orders that you will absolutely need to know (there are others, but these are the main two to learn and understand). The two order methods for placing a trade are called Market and Limit Orders. We discussed stop losses earlier to minimize potential losses, if you need more reference, go back Chapter 11 – Growth vs. Value Investing.

MARKET ORDER

A Market Order occurs when a customer wants to buy or sell their stock. The order is immediately executed at the best price available. This can be compared with a quick stop at the supermarket – get in, shop, and get out. Because the customer initiates the order, they also must specify the security and the size of the order. By using this type of order, execution and completion are certain.

LIMIT ORDER

A Limit Order is a situation where a customer only wants to buy or sell at a set price or higher. The order is only executed if the price is met, which is where the "limit" part comes in. There is a buy limit, which means the stock must be bought at a set price or lower. There is also a sell limit, which means that the stock must sell at a set price or higher. The customer specifies the security, size, and price. With all these limits and conditions, execution is not certain. An example of this can be found in the Walmart Rollback program; a customer may only be willing to buy a product if the price is lowered.

There's one more point here that I need to bring up for all investing (both value & growth) regarding if the market or stocks go into a downward crash. Before transitioning to growth investing, I want to explain how to take action to limit potential losses. It's a very simple tool to use that is available in every brokerage account (but not in a DRIP plan). It's a really cool investment tool called Stop Losses. T next natural question is what is a Stop Loss?

STOP LOSS

A stop loss is open trade placed in a brokerage account to cap potential losses. This is used as a protection in case something happens with a company or the stock market in general. **This only works with brokerage accounts, not accounts sponsored by major DRIP providers like Computershare and Wells Fargo Investment Services.** This tool will automatically trigger a sell at a specific price level if a stock begins to trade down or even goes into free-fall mode. This helps in those situations where the investor has no time to send in a trade to prevent further losses. To enter a Stop Loss on a brokerage account, follow these instructions:

1. Login to the brokerage account
2. Select Trading from the Tool Bar
3. Select Stocks
4. Under Transaction, select Sell from Holdings
5. Enter the symbol and quantity

6. Order Type - Stop (Do not select Sell Limit!!) See below on why

7. Enter a Price – Select a price that's comfortable taking the risk, suggested 15-30% below current market price or original purchase

8. Duration – Good till Canceled

9. Account Type – Enter Account Type

This will setup an automatic trigger to sell a position if the stock falls below the threshold setup in the price stop. This trigger will keep you protected from larger potential losses down the line in a future strategy. Now, let's discuss **Sell Stop Limit** for a minute as another option.

This is a very, very bad investment option that should have never been provided to investors because it just confuses investors. It's confusing because it's setup right next to "Sell Stop" (without the limit). The Sell Stop Limit works like this, using Stock A as an example:

- Stock A has a sell stop limit of 35.50 setup
- Stock A is trading at 40.00 at the beginning of the day

- Stock A announces earnings miss, and suddenly drops to 36, 35.75, 35.51, 35.45 and falls all the way to 31.25 at the end of the day
- The sell stop limit never triggers, investors lose more than intended because they don't trade on Wall Street and watch the channel everyday
- This is not what was supposed to happen
- That stinks!
- If using a simple Sell Stop instead, the sell would have triggered at 35.50 and it would have saved those points and more importantly, money

By understanding Sell Stop Limit and Sell Stop, it's much clearer which choice can alter the investment strategy and minimize potential losses. If nothing else, please remember: Don't use a Sell Stop Limit, Don't use a Sell Stop Limit, Don't use a Sell Stop Limit!

DEFENSIVE STOCKS

When the economy goes through up and down cycles, certain industries are more resistant to downturns that can help protect the portfolio in a recession. Just to name a few, companies that sell cigarettes, utilities, food, and gasoline are all classified as defensive stocks. Companies like this tend to remain stable during difficult conditions of the economy and can actually perform better than the market overall in times of economic uncertainty.

I want to make a quick distinction that defensive stocks are not defensive companies. **Defensive companies** like Northrop Grumman Corporation (NOC) and Lockheed Martin (LMT) make products used for national defense like missiles for example. On the other hand, **defensive stocks** (used in uncertainty and recession periods) are stocks like Exxon Mobile (XOM, gasoline), Philip Morris International (PM, cigarettes), and Kraft Foods Group (KRFT, foods). Some companies make missiles while others make everyday products.

FUTURES

This is a term heard on television, the internet, or generally anywhere to get news that includes financial data. Futures are used by professional traders to hedge against potential price movements in the future for hedging, trading, and investing. Similar to an option, the purchaser of the stock future agrees to buy or sell an investment at a future date at a future price. If the trader knew that coffee prices were going to increase significantly next year, and could lock in a current rate six months in advance, then they would be holding onto a valuable investment (could be sold later at a lower price). For example, if coffee was trading at $10.00 per pound, and an investor locked in a price of $12.00 per pound, and the price in six months rises to $15.00 per pound, that would make $3.00 per pound for X amount of purchases. Futures are used extensively in the airline industry to lock in fuel prices to keep costs down. Futures should be viewed, just as options, as a "stay away for now" when creating a plan to invest since they require another level of experience that's beyond our learning speed.

STOCK SPLITS

Stock splits are important to understand what they are and why they occur. I bring it up because it happened to me several times and I really didn't know what happened the first couple of times. For example, a few years back I wanted to know why one of my stocks suddenly dropped from a share price of $31.00 per share to $24.00 per share overnight without any negative news. Even more confusing is that my overall value didn't change, and yet the stock appeared to be down 23% overnight. Yes, I know, it can be confusing. These will occur in from time to time as companies adjust their market position. It's important to recognize their impact on the stock and dividends. A stock split is generally a company's attempt to improve marketability of their stock. Some quick facts about stock splits:

- No economic gain or loss for shareholders
- No change to company's market capitalization (total value)
- No change to shareholder's percentage of equity ownership
- No immediate change in or about personal tax liability

There are two types of stock splits, forward and reverse. An easy way to remember -

- ✓ Forward – more shares, lower price
- ✓ Reverse – less shares, higher price

In general, forward stock splits are perceived better for the marketability of the company and will normally result in a positive impact to the stock, such as an increase in stock price. Reverse stock splits have the exact opposite effect on the share price, meaning it could result in a loss. Dividends per share are adjusted accordingly depending on which way the split goes. Here's an example below:

Stocks	Stock Price (Before)	Dividend	Dividend Payment	Stock Split	Stock Price (New)	Dividend Payment)
Stock A	$100	4%	$4	2:1	$50	$2
Stock B	$20	5%	$1	1:2	$40	$2

In this example, Stock A performed a forward stock split and the 2:1 means 2 for 1. For every 1 share owned, the investor will now own 2 shares instead after the split occurs. If the investor owned 100 shares at $100 each ($10,000 market value), after the split, the investor would now own 200 shares at $50, make sense? The overall market value doesn't change from the $10,000. The complete opposite is with the reversal stock split of Stock B regarding the 1:2 (1 for 2) split. If the investor owned 100 shares at $20 price, after the split, the investor would now own 50 shares at $40. The total market value doesn't change from $2,000. **If anything remember,** (forward split) more shares with a lower price are better for a stock owned, than the reverse split.

DIVIDEND REINVESTMENT PLANS (DRIPS) INVESTING DIRECTLY USING A TRANSFER AGENT

Most of the plans covered in Computershare and EQ Shareowner are called Dividend Reinvestment Plans (or DRIP for short) plans or Direct Stock Purchase Plans (DSPP for short) plans. Both plan types act the same by allowing investors to invest directly with the company instead of on the open market in a brokerage account. I would say the biggest difference is that a DSPP doesn't require current ownership in the company to participate. Let's discuss both of these in brief:

- **DSPP** – These plans allow smaller retail investors (like you and me) to invest directly with a company for a very small cost (sometimes nothing!). The plans will also reinvest the dividend payouts at no cost to investors and allow investors to start participating without previously owning any shares in the stock.

- **DRIP** – As stated above, these plans are very similar to DSPP plans. Like DSPP, these plans are offered for little or no fees to buy except for ownership. A DRIP plan requires ownership of at least one share prior to investing; however, most will require to start with an initial investment to get around this minor detail required (which goes towards stock purchase). For the plans that do not offer this service, the investor would have to buy one share on the open market, transfer it to the agent like Computershare, and then the opportunity to purchase shares in the DRIP would become available.

For both plans, there are a few restrictions that need to be addressed. The fee to sell a stock is generally much higher (usually $25) per sale than that of a brokerage account. Once requesting a sale of stock, it generally takes two weeks for the entire sale to be completed, as opposed to a brokerage account. Remember, brokerage accounts will allow selling stock that day, and the proceeds become available after two days. Computershare or EQ Shareowner Online – These platforms only offer automatic investment plan option. The first noticeable option within Computershare and Wells Fargo are there are fewer options than Sharebuilder. There are over 1,000 different investment options here ranging from stocks, ETFs, and Real Estate Investment Trusts (REITs). The companies that are registered and are available for investments have outsourced their investment plans to Computershare and Wells Fargo for both internal and external investors that want to invest with them.

ETFS

VALUE ETFS –

iShares Large Cap Value (IUSV)

iShares Mid-Cap Value (IJJ)

iShares Small Cap Value (IJS)

iShares S&P 500 / Barra Value Index (IVE)

iShares S&P Midcap 400 / Barra Value (IJJ)

iShares S&P Smallcap 600 / Barra Value (IJS)

iShares Russell 1000 Value Index Ticker (IWD)

iShares Russell 2000 Value Index (IWN)

iShares Russell 3000 Value Index (IWW)

GROWTH ETFS –

iShares Large Cap Growth (IVV)

Guggenheim S&P MidCap 400 Pure Growth (RFG)

iShares S&P 500 / Barra Growth Index (IVW)

iShares S&P Mid Cap 400 / Barra Growth (IJK)

iShares S&P Small Cap 600 / Barra Growth (IJT)

iShares Russell 1000 Growth Index Ticker (IWF)

iShares Russell 2000 Growth Index (IWO)

iShares Russell 3000 Growth Index (IWZ)

Powershares Trust, Series 1, NASDAQ 100 (QQQ)

BLENDED ETFS (MIXED)

iShares Mega Cap Mixed (ITOT)

Vanguard Large Cap Mixed (VIG) Dividend Appreciation

iShares Large Cap Mixed (IVV)

iShares Mid-Cap Mixed (IJH)

iShares Small Cap Mixed (IJR)

Vanguard Total Stock Market Mixed (VTI)

REVERSE ETFS (INVERSE)

Short QQQ NASDAQ (PSQ)

Short Down 30 (DOG)

Short S&P 500 (SH)

Short Mid-Cap (MYY)

Short Small Cap Russell (RWM)

EXPLORING BONDS MORE IN DETAIL

- Bond Types & Ratings
- Zero Coupon – These bonds pay no periodic interest; issued at a deep discount; matures at par value; have no reinvestment risk; attractive for planning for specific investment goal (college funding, retirement property); not good for cash flow
- U.S. Treasuries – Listed below in the chart
- Maturity – The measure expressed in years of a fixed income security's price sensitivity to changes in interest rates. The greater the duration, the greater percentage

volatility. The maturity rates for Treasury Bonds are listed below by treasury type.

- Default & Risk – Bonds by nature are inherintently lower in terms of risk. Their risk of default is completely measured below in the second chart by their rating. AAA is near perfect against default whereas a C+ Corporate Bond has a much higher risk of default.

	U.S. Treasuries		
	Treasury Bills (T-Bills)	Treasury Notes (T-Notes)	Treasury Bonds (T-Bonds)
Matures	Up to one year	Between 2-10 years	Greater than 10 years
Denominations	$100 multiples	$100 multiples	$100 multiples
Interest	At discount, trades with accrued interest	Stated annual, paid semi-annual	Stated annual, paid semi-annual
How Sold	Weekly auction	At periodic Auction	At periodic Auction

		Rating Agency	
		S&P / Fitch	Moody's
	Low	AAA	Aaa
		AA	Aa
Risk Rating		A	A
		BBB	Baa
		BB	Ba
	High	B	B

Further Differentiate		+/-	1,2,3

		Rating Agency	
		S&P	Moody's
	Low	SP-1	MIG 1
Risk		Sp-2	MIG 2
		Sp-3	MIG 3
	High		MIG 4

ESTABLISHING DIFFERENT ACCOUNT TYPES –

- Individual Account – Single person responsible for all account transactions. Most accounts fall under this category
- Transfer on Death (TOD) – This is similar to an Individual Account but can be setup as a Joint Account. It's used to automate transfer of securities to a named beneficiary without going through probate
- Joint Accounts – Account with two or more owners to manage and operate the holdings
  - Joint Tenants with Rights of Survivorship (JTWROS)
    - Common for spouses

268

- One spouse dies; ownership passes to survivor without probate with death cert.
  - ○ Joint Tenancy in Common (JTTEN-COM)
    - Common for business partners
    - One partner dies; decedent's portion goes to their estate
- Trust Account – Acts like an individual or joint account depending on the trust agreement. Great way to avoid probate upon the account designation.
- College savings plans
  - ○ ESA (Educational Savings Accounts) – College plan that can be withdrawn tax free during K-12 years for educational expenses. Has $2,000 contribution limit annually.
  - ○ 529 plans – Used more extensively for college students and saving. 529 plans don't post limits on contributions and are much easier to use.
    - Both accounts can be used as a source to reduce taxes on college savings
- Retirement accounts

- ○ IRA – Individual Retirement Account; use as an after taxes investment account type to save money for retirement. Tax credit for using upon deposit, taxed when withdrawn later in life.

- ○ Roth IRA – Similar to IRA, however when removing monies later at Required Minimum Distribution time, the money is not taxed upon withdrawals

- ○ 401K – This is an employer sponsored plan for employees to save and invest money for their retirement savings

- ○ 403B – U.S. tax-advantaged retirement savings plan available for public education

If still interesting in more information, take a look at any of these investing resources below to further educate yourself on trends within investing.

ADDITIONAL INVESTING RESOURCES

- Periodicals – Magazine or newspaper articles regarding investing

- Value Line – One of the top investment research firms within Wall Street

- Standard & Poors (S&P) – Another top investment research firm that publishes investment research and analysis

- Wall Street Journal – A top of the line newspaper that has a very thorough section dedicated daily to Wall Street and its daily actions

- Morningstar – This is an independent research firm that is most closely tied to mutual fund ratings based on history and quality of the overall fund (management, sector, composition)

EVEN MORE INVESTMENT RESOURCES (FREE STUFF)

- Podcasts – I really like the S&A Investment series and the Wall Street Unplugged Radio Podcast featuring Frank Curzio. The one I listen to the most is by Frank Curzio. He does a really good job of breaking down the markets and not getting too detailed to confuse people. Check it out on iTunes and subscribe.

- 10-K, 10-Q – SEC required public tax documents on annual & quarterly reports

- CNNMoney – This channel revolves daily around the stock market and anything Wall Street related to provide up to the minute updates

- Conference Calls – Each public company holds a conference calls with investors that are FREE to attend and give the exact direction of the firm

- How to select other investment books – Read the first 20 pages. See what books speak to your interests, but also ones that conflict with your point of view.

  a. Here are a few extra books that I really like and have read –

     i. All About ETFs – Scott Frush - Amazon Link

     ii. The Neatest Little Guide to Stock Market Investing – Jason Kelly – Amazon Link

     iii. Cracking the Code – Understand and Profit from the Biotech Revolution That will Transform our Lives and Generate Fortune – Mellon, Chalabi – Amazon Link

iv. The Little Book That Makes You Rich – Louis Navellier – <u>Amazon Link</u>

v. <u>The Complete Guide to Investing in Bonds and Bond Funds: How to Earn High Rates of Return Safely – Martha Maeda</u> – **<u>Amazon Link</u>**

Terms used in the book/conventions

Working Capital = Current Assets − Current Liabilities

Current Ratio = (Current Assets − Inventory) / Current Liabilities

Current Yield = Annual Dividend / Current Stock Price. This is also called the dividend yield or stock yield and is the rate of return stated as a percentage.

EPS = Earnings Per Share, calculated from a company's quarterly or annual profits divided by the number of common shares outstanding − (Net Income − Preferred Dividends) / Common Shares Outstanding

Forward Stock Split − Company increases outstanding shares by issuing shares. For Example − 2:1 (2 for 1), lower price, resulting in more shares

Reverse Stock Split − Company decreases outstanding shares. Example − 1:2 (1 for 2), higher price

APR or Annual Percentage Rate – The interest rate charged on credit card balances expressed in a standard annual rate. The rate is applied each month and compounded to provide a monthly rate, where the rate is applied to the outstanding balance.

ADR, American Depository Receipt – A receipt for foreign securities held in a U.S. bank located in the foreign country.

10-K – Annual report that publicly traded companies are required to file with the Securities and Exchange Commission (SEC). The report has an overview of operations and audited financial statements signed by the CEO of the company. Financial statements include the income statement, balance sheet, and statement of cash flows.

10-Q – This is a quarterly report filed by public companies with the SEC by 45 days after the close of each of the first three quarters of the year. This roles directly up into the 10-K for the annual statement.

Bear Market – Extended period of the stock market where stock prices fall across all market caps, including major stock index averages such as the DJIA and S&P 500.

Bull Market – Extended period of the stock market where stock prices rise above across all market caps, including major stock index averages such as the DJIA and S&P 500.

CD or Certificate of Deposit – A deposit at a bank institution with a fixed rate of interest and maturity date. The CD must stay at the bank for set time duration and early withdrawals generally signal a penalty imposed by the bank on customer.

Defensive Stocks – Stocks that traditionally perform well in a down (or bear) market. These stocks include examples such as utility, food, and energy stocks.

Dollar-cost averaging – Method of investing with a fixed sum at the same intervals (ex. Monthly). This is used to minimize market risk by buying shares at multiple levels in the marketplace routinely (at high and low prices).

Dow Jones Industrial Average – Dow Jones Industrial Average (DJIA) that was created in 1896. This average is made up of 30 large cap stocks from various sectors that make up the average

DRIP or Dividend Reinvestment Plan – A plan that buys shares of a company (sometimes directly) and the shareholder has the option to reinvest the dividends at little to no cost.

DSPP or Direct Stock Purchase Plan – Similar to a DRIP, these plans allows the investor to buy shares directly from the company and option to reinvest dividends at little to no cost.

Earnings Estimates – Estimates made by industry analysts that follow the company stock for future quarterly and annual earnings.

Earnings Surprise – This is a situation when a company announces their quarterly earnings and the announced earnings exceeds what is projected by analysts.

ETF (Exchange Traded Fund) – Similar to Mutual Funds, this represents a fixed basket of stocks generally linked to a stock index or class of stocks. The ETF trades just like a stock can be bought and sold with the same instructions / restrictions as a common stock trade.

Fed or Federal Reserve Board – The Board of Governor's to the Federal Reserve System. The current chairman is Janet L Yellen as of 2015.

Fixed Income Investment – Investments that offer a fixed rate of interest or return and must be redeemed at maturity to realize full value as agreed upon. Examples would be bonds or CDs.

Float – The number of outstanding shares of a publicly owned company.

Fundamentals – This refers to specific characteristics of a company to establish the company's overall health. These characteristics include items found on the 10-K such as the financial data (income statement, balance sheet, and cash flow statement), products or services offered, and their management team.

Growth ratio – Use the growth rate of the stock's EPS divided by its P/E ratio.

Hedge – Investment strategy that involves reducing risk of the portfolio by owning investments contrary to the rest of the portfolio. Example – owning a reverse ETF to offset potential losses to portfolio if the market tumbles.

Industry group – Group of stocks in similar business. Example – health care companies that manufacture and sell health care products like JNJ, MRK, MDT.

Institutional Investor – Large organization that invest in large amounts of money (billions of dollars) in securities. Examples – Mutual Fund, Pension Fund, Insurance Company, Hedge Fund

Long – Owning a security for the purposes of it appreciating in value. For example, if you are long JNJ, you own shares of JNJ generally over 1 calendar year.

Margin – Type 2 account in a brokerage account. This account is used as a memorandum account that records a customer's excess margin and buying power. Excess funds in the margin account come from several sources: Sale of security proceeds, market value appreciation, dividends and cash or securities in response to a margin call. Margin may also be reflective of the company's profit margin.

Market cap rotation – The movement of different market capitalization that fall in and out of favor with the market.

Market Cap (Capitalization) – The number of outstanding shares of a company multiplied by the current stock price. Measures the total value of a company.

Morningstar ratings – One to Five star rating given by Morningstar, Inc. to portray a mutual fund's risk adjusted performance. Morningstar is an investment research company.

Moving average – The average price of a company's stock over an explicit date range usually plotted for graphical analysis.

NAV (Net Asset Value) – The market price of one share of an open ended mutual fund. NAV is computed daily by subtracting liabilities from the value of the fund's investments, divided by number of outstanding shares.

Option – A contract that gives the holder the right to buy or sell shares on the underlying security at a specific price within a specific time frame. Call option is the right to buy; Put option is the right to sell.

Option Premium – The price of the option contract the buyer must pay to own the option.

Out of the Money Contract – An option that the strike price is greater than or less than the market price of the security.

Penny Stocks or Over the Counter Stocks – Stocks that are traded less than $5 per share, also traded on "Pink Sheets". I referred to these in the micro-caps section.

Price to book value – A company's current stock price divided by its book value; compare the stock's total market value it its book value (total asset – total liabilities).

REIT or Real Estate Investment Trust – An entity that invests in real estate or loans secured by real estate and issues shares.

Relative P/E – A stock's price to earnings ratio compared with its own history.

Resistance Level – A price level at which a stock normally stops rising and either moves sideways or reverses direction.

S&P 500 – Market index of 500 major US Public companies, weighted for market cap. The index is used to measure the performance of the entire US domestic stock market.

SEC or Securities & Exchange Commission – The U.S. agency that regulates the securities industry.

Sell signal – A technical term that indicates the beginning of a downward trend on a stock, signaling to sell the stock.

Short selling – selling shares of a borrowed security that are expected to decline in the price with the intention of buying the shares at a lower price to replace borrowed shares. For example – if you expect AAPL to decline over the next six months, you would short AAPL, borrow the shares from your broker, and buy them at a lower price to realize a profit.

SPDR or Spider – original ETFs that mimic the different indexes.

Spread – the difference between the big price and the ask price for a stock purchase or sale.

Stock Index – Represents a class of stocks within an industry or asset class.

Strike Price – the price per share for which the underlying security may be purchased or sold by the option holder.

Support level – A price level at which a stock normally stops falling and either moves sideways or reverses direction.

Technical analysis – study of past trading patterns of a security in an attempt to predict future movements of the stock, generally uses lots of chart analysis.

Trade – purchase or sale of a stock.

Undervalued stock – stock that's price is considered undervalued. The P/E ratio is less than the EPS future growth rate used by value investors.

Volatility – measure of a stock's price fluctuations. High volatility means frequent and large swings in the price, whereas low volatility means small price fluctuations.

Volume – the number of shares traded in a security or the entire market in a given period.

www.ingramcontent.com/pod-product-compliance
Lightning Source LLC
Chambersburg PA
CBHW030942240526
45463CB00016B/1248